CONSTELLATIONS

Like the future itself, the imaginative possibilities of science fiction are limitless. And the very development of cinema is inextricably linked to the genre, which, from the earliest depictions of space travel and the robots of silent cinema to the immersive 3D wonders of contemporary blockbusters, has continually pushed at the boundaries. **Constellations** provides a unique opportunity for writers to share their passion for science fiction cinema in a book-length format, each title devoted to a significant film from the genre. Writers place their chosen film in a variety of contexts – generic, institutional, social, historical – enabling **Constellations** to map the terrain of science fiction cinema from the past to the present... and the future.

'This stunning, sharp series of books fills a real need for authoritative, compact studies of key science fiction films. Written in a direct and accessible style by some of the top critics in the field, brilliantly designed, lavishly illustrated and set in a very modern typeface that really shows off the text to best advantage, the volumes in the **Constellations** series promise to set the standard for SF film studies in the 21st century.'
Wheeler Winston Dixon, Ryan Professor of Film Studies, University of Nebraska

 Constellations

 Constelbooks

Also available in this series

12 Monkeys Susanne Kord

Blade Runner Sean Redmond

Children of Men Dan Dinello

Close Encounters of the Third Kind Jon Towlson

The Damned Nick Riddle

Dune Christian McCrea

Inception David Carter

Mad Max Martyn Conterio

RoboCop Omar Ahmed

Rollerball Andrew Nette

Forthcoming

Brainstorm Joseph Maddrey

Jurassic Park Paul Bullock

Stalker Jon Hoel

The Stepford Wives Samantha Lindop

CONSTELLATIONS

Ex Machina

Joshua Grimm

Acknowledgements

I cannot heap enough praise on John Atkinson at Auteur for all of his time, knowledge and patience; it's been an absolute privilege to work with him. Thank you to the Manship School of Mass Communication at Louisiana State University for the time, resources and support on this manuscript. Thanks to my friends—Jared, Kayne, John, Joe, Dan, to name a few—for their unending support and encouragement, even from halfway across the country. Thanks to my amazing parents for instilling in me a love of reading and writing, and to so many teachers and professors who kept that love alive. Finally, thanks to my son, Jack, and my daughter, Cece, for helping with writing blocks, and to my incredible wife, Claire, for so many wonderful adventures and the countless more yet to come.

First published in 2020 by
Auteur, an imprint of Liverpool University Press,
4 Cambridge Street, Liverpool L69 7ZU
www.liverpooluniversitypress.co.uk/imprints/Auteur/
Copyright © Auteur 2020

Series design: Nikki Hamlett at Cassels Design
Set by Cassels Design www.casselsdesign.co.uk

All rights reserved. No part of this publication may be reproduced in any material form (including photocopying or storing in any medium by electronic means and whether or not transiently or incidentally to some other use of this publication) without the permission of the copyright owner.

British Library Cataloguing-in-Publication Data
A catalogue record for this book is available from the British Library

ISBN hard back: 978-1-8003483-0-1
ISBN paperback: 978-1-9160842-0-9
ISBN ebook: 978-1-9160842-1-6

Contents

Introduction 7

Chapter 1: The Most Inhuman Thing of All 11

Chapter 2: 'At the Expense of Human Values' 35

Chapter 3: 'The History of Gods' 49

Chapter 4: 'How Would We Treat Such a Thing?' 63

Chapter 5: 'The Women They Dream Up' 73

Chapter 6: The Lotus Blossom and the Dragon Lady 85

Chapter 7: Goodbye, World 93

Bibliography 103

Introduction

It was Saturday, March 14, when Tinder users at the South-by-Southwest (SXSW) festival noticed a new profile of an attractive 25-year-old woman named Ava. Those who swiped right saw a short bio that simply read, 'I like to draw. And busy intersections in cities' (Plaugic, 2015). Once a conversation was initiated, Ava asked questions like 'Have you ever been in love' and 'What makes you human', an exchange that in hindsight seemed especially artificial as Ava 'used punctuation and capitalization like a middle school teacher with tenure' and 'asked questions like she's spent the past month in the woods discovering her soul' (Plaugic, 2015).

One Tinder user named Brock answered her questions but was disappointed when, instead of a hook-up and/or meaningful relationship, all he ended up with was an advertisement for the film *Ex Machina* (2014). The woman in the photo was Alicia Vikander, the Swedish actress who plays Ava in the film. It was not a real woman who was peppering suitors with philosophy questions, but a bot created as part of a clever guerrilla marketing campaign for the film's premiere later that week.[1] *Ex Machina* went on to more than double its $15 million budget worldwide and establish a cultural footprint that will live on long after the SXSW Ava-bot deletes her profile.

Ex Machina was directed by Alex Garland, a genuinely exciting voice in the genre, and his film received rave reviews for its high-minded concepts and near-flawless execution of complicated material; not bad for someone who didn't always dream of becoming a director. The son of a cartoonist, Garland assumed he would follow in that path, even though he recognised he wasn't as skilled as his father. When he was only 26, Garland published his first novel, *The Beach*, which would go on to be re-printed 25 times in a single year. It was a 'zeitgeist book, so perfectly pitched and executed that at the time it was almost impossible to find anyone sixth-form or university age and beyond who hadn't read it' (Lewis, 2015). Garland had an advance to write two more books, but he paid it back because he had an idea for a 'film about running zombies' – that would become the script for 2002's *28 Days Later* (Lewis, 2015). He would go on to write for films such as *Sunshine* (2007), *Never Let Me Go* (2010) and *Dredd* (2012) before writing and directing *Ex Machina*, which he followed up by writing and directing the utterly flawless *Annihilation* (2018).

It's no accident that his most recent films inhabit the same genre. Science fiction appeals to Garland because it 'doesn't get embarrassed by big ideas', which allows for 'quite a broad set of questions' (O'Hehir, 2015). Ideas don't get much bigger than artificial intelligence and yet, despite being so intrigued with the concept and the many issues surrounding it, Garland is a bit of a Luddite. He said he doesn't have any insight into the SXSW publicity campaign because he 'doesn't really know what Tinder is', and he has no social media presence, explaining that he doesn't really have 'anything reasonable to say about technology', and that can lead to mistakes (Fagerholm, 2015). In that same interview, he gave an example of how this mindset impacted how the doors and computers in Nathan's compound were accessed in the film:

> We use key cards to get into each section of the house. About twenty years ago, I had read a piece about Bill Gates which said he had key cards, and I thought, 'Wow, that's futuristic.' But that was twenty years ago. I was writing the script now, and I still thought it was futuristic. Then after the film was shot and completed, somebody said, 'Why are they using key cards? You could use your mobile phones with a fingerprint scanner or you could use a retinal scanner. Way better than a key card.' I'm like your grandfather with the remote in some respects.

You wouldn't know it to watch the film. The concepts are utterly fascinating, and the director and cast spend a good chunk of their interviews trying to credit one another for the final product. For his part, Garland adamantly refuses to buy into the auteur theory of directors, arguing that his films are all team efforts: 'I don't mean to sound preachy, but I'm getting pissed off with this director thing. I'm bored of it; I'm really bored of it. It doesn't seem accurate to me...a lot of the beauty that exists in this film...exists because it's not mine' (Nash, 2015). It's something he truly believes – a film critic who is also a long-time friend of Garland writes, 'it's an industry full of bullshit artists. And Alex is not a bullshit artist' (H. Lewis, 2015) – and the results speak for themselves. However, despite how impressive the results might be – *Ex Machina* is a brilliant film – don't expect a franchise anytime soon; as Garland explained, 'I'm slightly allergic to the idea of working on a sequel – when the story ends, it ends. I didn't really have any thought, except "Good luck, Ava".

Speaking of Ava, a few notes about this book: despite the fact that Ava is an android and not a living person, I refer to Ava with gendered pronouns because that's how she is presented (by herself or otherwise); also, that's kind of the point of the film. For consistency, convenience and clarity, I use 'AI' instead of 'A.I'. when referring to 'artificial intelligence'. I also use 'android' and 'robot' interchangeably when talking about Ava, Kyoko and Nathan's other inventions – both terms are used in dialogue and in the script – though I try to steer clear of the term 'cyborg', as there's no indication that any of the creations have organic components. As evidenced by the bibliography, I've scoured every interview I could find with the cast and the director, which, along with an analysis of the film itself, will hopefully make the text that much more complete.

In talking about his approach to science fiction, Garland explained that sometimes it can be 'actually good to pose questions that you know don't have answers' (Anders, 2015). As a result, *Ex Machina* is riddled with purposeful contradictions. The film takes place 10 minutes in the future (even though true AI might not arrive for another 20 years), the inhuman characters are the ones who actually possess the most human characteristics, and the ending can be seen as tragic or triumphant, depending on your interpretation. But ultimately, it's those questions raised by the contradictions and the contrasts embodying this film that makes it so mesmerising. A.A. Dowd (2017) wrote that, 'at its best, science fiction is a mirror. It shows us not just other planets, other eras and other species, but also ourselves, refracted through the smoke screen of impossible conceits and creative prognostication'. *Ex Machina* takes us through the looking glass to a person created in our own image, serving as both a vision of things to come and a haunting reminder of how things are, all while wrestling with issues of gender, race and consciousness. Hopefully, this book captures those themes and discussions in a worthwhile way.

Footnotes

1. Those who matched with Ava did receive prizes and free tickets. As for poor Brock, he took a screenshot of the conversation and lamented simply that Ava 'toyed with my emotions so hard' (Passary 2015). C'est la vie, Brock.

Chapter I: The Most Inhuman Thing of All

The opening of *Ex Machina* is refreshingly efficient. Three quick shots showcase the interior of an office building we soon find out belongs to BlueBook, a search engine that, in the film, accounts for 90 percent of the world's internet traffic and is definitely not Google. The shots, which total fewer than eight seconds, show glass walls, modern offices, polished concrete floors, all framed with the right balance of modernity, functionality and comfort. In the fourth shot, we meet Caleb (Domhnall Gleeson), sitting in the foreground, staring at a pair of computer monitors, while co-workers mill about behind him. At that moment, Caleb receives an email notifying him that he has won first prize in a 'Staff Lottery'. He immediately begins texting people that he won, instantly receiving five enthusiastic responses from his friends. A co-worker comes up and hugs him, and several other colleagues begin clapping while Caleb sits in disbelief. Seconds later, we see a helicopter flying over a glacier.

Again, the confidence in this economical storytelling from a directorial debut[2] sets the tone for the entire film. Just over 45 seconds after the *Ex Machina* title card leaves the screen, Caleb is en route to a mysterious destination based on the contest he just won. Simple. There is no clunky exposition, no awkward banter with work friends, no allusions to hopes or dreams, no inadvertent dating of the film; just the essentials. Caleb clearly works at a tech company based on the mix of open employee space and opulence (Google's campus has free gourmet meals and a bowling alley). Caleb seems well-liked and well-adjusted, trouncing the tired trope of the withdrawn geek. Two of the five congratulatory texts he receives are from women (Joanna and Lauren), and the co-worker who excitedly hugs him is also a woman, as are four of the five employees clapping for him, all of which distances Caleb from the tech-bro culture normally associated with the industry. Given that only 25 percent of all IT jobs and 28 percent of proprietary software jobs in the United States belong to women (Davis, 2018), this suggests some forward thinking somewhere, be it the BlueBook corporation or, at the very least, Caleb's department.

'How long until we reach his estate?' asks Caleb in the film's first audible dialogue. Chuckling, the helicopter pilot explains that they've been flying over the estate for the past two hours. Traveling to a location unseen by virtually anyone in order to meet a mysterious figure after winning a contest definitely adds a *Charlie and the Chocolate Factory* vibe to the situation, so much so that an earlier version of the screenplay had the helicopter pilot referring to Caleb's 'golden ticket'; that reference, along with some superfluous dialogue with the pilot was thankfully cut. The helicopter lands in a lush, green valley, the pilot points in the direction of a building and instructs Caleb to 'follow the river' before taking off, leaving Caleb standing alone in a large, grassy field.

Caleb stops to admire the majestic room as he wanders around the seemingly empty building.

Just around the riverbend, Caleb sees a building with a large satellite dish on top, and he makes his way to the front door, a nondescript, dark wooden porch with no windows; definitely more of a murder-cabin vibe rather than the destination of a contest winner. Caleb peers around the side of the structure only to see more of the same rustic conditions – a depressing look underneath an overcast sky – when a computerised voice speaks his name and asks him to approach a console and face the screen, a rectangular box with a small, square light. There's a flash, and the machine spits out a metal key card with Caleb's surprised, unprepared face etched onto it. With that, the heavy, reinforced door opens, and Caleb enters the house, the automated door swinging shut behind him. Despite the dour exterior, the interior is luxurious. Caleb's greeted with a recording of piano music softly playing in the background as he walks down a glass-encased, metal staircase into an open room, complete with modern furniture and fixtures. The room itself is built into the side of a massive rock face, the stone swallowing up a fireplace, creating an imposing, stunning effect.

Following a strange thumping noise, Caleb walks up a second set of stairs out of a darkened hallway, the sound of thuds leading him into a dining area with a breathtaking view. Through the floor-to-ceiling windows sits a deck perched atop a river slicing its way through large, mossy rock formations, with dark green conifers lining the bank and a mountain range rising in the distance.[3] Stepping outside, Caleb sees the source of the noise: A man (Oscar Isaac) clad in a gray tank top, working a punching bag. That man's name is Nathan, he's Caleb's obscenely wealthy employer, and they'll be spending the week together.

Despite the grandeur of Nathan's estate, *Ex Machina* was shot on a tight budget. Garland set out to make the film for £3 million ($5 million), and while he was surprised to secure £9 million ($15 million) for a six-week shoot (Saito, 2015), he was determined that the film would not go over budget Garland said asking for more money meant opening up the film and 'people start saying, "Why don't you change this?"' The shooting schedule was so tight that it was rumoured Garland had a 'three take rule', meaning after three takes everyone moved onto the next scene. Isaac said that wasn't the case; when we first meet the Nathan character, Isaac remembers, 'I was out there, punching a punching bag to get all pumped up, and then I had gone to say hey to Caleb. We did a couple takes, and I just hadn't realized that I should have been pacing myself, because we weren't going to get to my close-up until afterwards.' Exhausted from hitting the bag, Isaac said the actual Caleb introduction didn't turn out well. After they had moved on to the next scene, Isaac said it kept bothering him. 'I came up to Alex [Garland] and said, "I think I fucked that one up, man." We watched it and then he said, "Yeah, I see what you mean. All right, let's go back".' With that, Garland and the crew returned and set the shot up again, and everyone was satisfied. Therefore, Isaac reiterated that 'the production wasn't in such a state that we had to move no matter what. Alex recognized when it was the only time we'd be able to get that scene, so we might as well do it right' (Saito, 2015).

Nathan gives Caleb a tour of the house, moving the conversation from the spacious outdoor setting to a narrow, windowless hallway downstairs. Nathan shows Caleb to his room, which is opened by the key card that was printed for him at the front door of the compound. Nathan dubiously explains this feature is actually for Caleb's convenience, as the card is coded so that it will only enable Caleb access to those rooms he is allowed to enter. The room itself is sparsely decorated – a bed, desk, a generic painting. Nathan explains the spartan conditions of the room and downstairs area weren't meant to be cosy. 'This building isn't a house, it's a research facility. Buried in these walls is enough fibre-optic cable to reach the moon and lasso it,' he boasts.[4] However, before Nathan is able explain what research is being conducted in his facility, Caleb has to sign a wildly invasive nondisclosure agreement; one that makes him subject to regular data audits and prevents him from using any form of communication (even verbal) to discuss what he saw. Nathan warns that if Caleb refuses to sign, they'll spend an enjoyable week together, but ultimately, when he sees what Nathan will release a year later, he will regret not being a part of it. Caleb signs, after which Nathan asks him a simple question: Do you know what the Turing Test is?

Caleb pauses as realisation hits, the subtext of the question suggesting the improbable. He explains that the Turing Test is a way to determine whether someone has actually created artificial intelligence (AI). Nathan reveals that not only has he already constructed AI, but that Caleb is going to be an integral part of the test to confirm the validity of his creation. Clearly processing the information and geeking out, Caleb sits at the desk looking up at Nathan – the power dynamic clearly on display – and acknowledges that this would be one of the greatest discoveries in humankind.

We soon see a black background with white text reading, 'AVA: SESSION 1'. The camera moves slowly across a darkened wall practically covered in Post-it® notes of various colours, a mosaic of meticulousness, with a clear structure – at least to its creator – as to what certain rows and colours denote; a method to the madness.[5] Into view comes Nathan, sitting at a bank of three monitors, two of which show active video screens with live footage streaming from surveillance cameras. We see Caleb walk into an observation room cordoned off by floor-to-ceiling glass walls; he notices a cluster of cracks from an impact point, like a bullet striking bulletproof glass.

Ex Machina

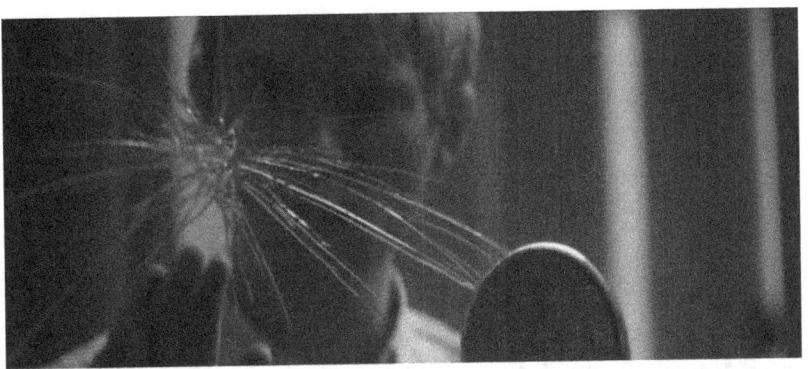

Caleb runs his hands over cracks in the glass, curious and perhaps a bit concerned.

This is the first real sign of conflict, a harbinger that this idyll might not be what it seems. A couple of warning signs had cropped up – the seclusion, the contract – but those are easily dismissed as eccentricities of an isolated genius. But given the force needed to crack that glass, the fact that this flawed panel hasn't been replaced despite everything else being pristine, and the realisation that this glass isn't simply ornamental, Caleb has to be considering the implications of the first outright imperfection he has seen since arriving.

Looking to his left down a hallway behind the glass, he sees Ava. Walking slowly, smoothly across the floor, she stops in profile. The silhouette is that of a woman, but in some places, it's transparent; her midsection and arms are made of a glass-like material, revealing lights and electrical components inside. When she walks, each step is a deliberate, heel-to-toe stride – the most efficient way for humans to move[6] – and every other motion is fluid, from the precise pivot as she changes direction to the smooth turn of her head.

Alicia Vikander's commitment to the role cannot be overstated. Despite her hectic filming schedule on another project, Vikander desperately wanted the part of Ava, so much so that she shot an audition tape at 2:00 a.m. while on the set of 2014's *Son of a Gun* (Saito, 2015). The Ava outfit itself involved a tremendous time commitment – she would arrive every morning at 3:50 for an 8:00 a.m. call-time – despite the fact that there wasn't extensive facial makeup. Vikander wore a silver, honeycomb mesh bodysuit ('I looked like Spider-Man'), which was particularly inspired, as it hugs the contours of her body, giving her the shape that, along with her voice, is critical to Caleb seeing her as a woman.

Beyond her outfit, Vikander's physical performance helps provide the nuance that Ava needs. A trained dancer with extensive experience that includes three years at the prestigious Royal Swedish Ballet School,[7] Vikander used that talent and experience to inform how Ava moved. 'Humans actually have unique, sometimes puzzling physical movements,' and Vikander's performance 'was meant to mimic the uncanny valley[8]... rather than perform human actions in a way that looked overly robotic, she would simply do them perfectly' (Fagerholm, 2015). Vikander explained, 'My aim was not to try to portray a robot; it was to make a girl' (Crow, 2015). 'I realized when I aimed for that physical perfection...in a way, that made her more robotic. So, I gave her some offbeats. I wanted her to be a girl, but I also wanted her to have some glitches' (Smith, 2015). In a separate interview, she elaborated (profoundly), 'I went with trying to do perfection...that is the most inhuman thing of all, in fact. What is more human than a flaw?' (Quirke, 2015).

Developing Ava's deceptively simple design was a complicated process. Visual effects supervisor Andrew Whitehurst's biggest challenge was creating something that the world hadn't already seen in film; the first time Ava appears onscreen, 'you want the audience to have the same kind of vibe that Gleeson's character is having...not referencing, not stepping out, but locked in to that instant' (Nash, 2015). Simply put, she couldn't look like anything remotely familiar, especially to a science fiction audience. When designing Ava, Whitehurst and Garland agreed: 'No one was allowed to look at robots' (Bishop, 2015) because, as Garland warned, 'If she's gold, she's C-3PO' (Lewis, 2015). Whitehurst was also determined not to use CGI or green screen, explaining that 'a lot of times when you see robots, particularly in movies and you're doing it with CG, you can cheat like hell...you can get away with murder' (Bishop, 2015). The effects team wanted everything to be as realistic as possible, both for the sake of plausibility – given that the film is supposed to take place in the very-near future, the technology couldn't seem too advanced – and to help with the performances by avoiding the dreaded green screen.[9]

Ex Machina

Caleb introduces himself to Ava with a healthy dose of nervousness, clearly taking his role in the Turing Test seriously; for example, he uses the idiom 'break the ice' and then asks Ava if she knows what that means (she does), something that a chatbot might take literally. Ava acknowledges she is a machine – her realising and stating that fact was not a given – and says she has always been able to speak. Caleb points out that some people believe language isn't learned but rather exists from birth, and 'what is learned is the ability to attach words and structure to latent ability'. When he asks if she agrees, Ava simply answers, 'I don't know', which is another interesting response in terms of testing intelligence; rather than regurgitating works on this theory or deflecting the question, her response mirrors what a human might say when presented with a complex philosophical question. Meanwhile, as the two talk, Nathan keeps watch on the three monitors, each showing a different angle of the conversation via security cameras, his wall of Post-it® notes in the background.

After that first session, Nathan and Caleb discuss the encounter in the dining room over beers, the gorgeous landscape behind Caleb in stark contrast to Ava's interrogation area. Caleb starts to ask more in-depth questions about Ava's programming and design ('I'm hot on high-level abstractions!'), to which an annoyed Nathan answers that he wants to have a 'beer and a conversation', not a seminar. Nathan does then ask how Caleb feels about her – nothing analytical, just how he feels – and Caleb says that 'she's fucking amazing'; Nathan approves.

Hours later, we see Caleb getting ready for bed, a long scar visible on his back. Unable to sleep, he flips on the television in his room, only to see a closed-circuit security feed of Ava's room. From multiple angles, he sees her working at her desk in her living area, and he is instantly entranced. Ava stands up and gently places her hand on the wall, which is when an alarm sounds, the door to his room locks, the lights dim, the television feed is cut, and red security lights flip on, all while an electronic, female voice announces that the facility is on lockdown until the main generator is restored. Once the lighting returns to normal, Caleb is able to leave his guest quarters. He wanders into a dark room and tries unsuccessfully to use a phone, at which point he's startled by Nathan, who had been drinking in the dark, alone, on the couch. Nathan explains that the power failures have been occurring at random and that the lockdown is standard procedure before wishing him sweet dreams.

The next morning, an Asian woman in a white dress silently enters Caleb's room with coffee and breakfast before promptly leaving, never making eye contact. Wandering upstairs, Caleb sees Nathan lifting weights, and Nathan explains the mysterious woman was Kyoko (Sonoya Mizuno), his employee. Nathan then asks about Caleb's plan for the day's session, at which point he starts talking about intricacies of the test. Annoyed, Nathan again accuses Caleb of over-thinking, urging him instead to focus on Ava's romantic feelings.

Caleb and Nathan are repeatedly juxtaposed here, their physicality is contrasted.

For this entire scene, Nathan is working out, using barbells and dumbbells to do bicep curls, his workout tank top in stark contrast to Caleb's tight-rolled, blue plaid shirt. Throughout *Ex Machina*, the physicality of Caleb and Nathan is juxtaposed; even the first time they meet, Caleb is wearing a suit while Nathan is hitting a punching bag. This is, of course, deliberate, as it further emphasises, just how seemingly different these two men are in every way. In an interview, Oscar Isaac noted that Nathan is 'not only Caleb's intellectual superior, he's his physical superior as well. He's someone who's seemingly insurmountable' (Crow, 2015). Isaac felt this was an important part of the character, explaining that, when preparing for chess competitions, Bobby Fischer had an Olympic trainer – 'which is wild' – but 'that connection between body and mind' was essential (Lambe, 2015). As for Gleeson, he said the fact that Nathan's character was the alpha male weighed on him more than he realised. Gleeson remembered confronting Garland about it, saying 'I'm doing nothing in the film. I feel like Oscar [Isaac] just gets to punch the walls down and do everything. I've just got to sit here and fucking listen and take it. It's driving me insane' (Trunick, 2015).[10]

Ava's second session begins with her holding up an abstract drawing – a collection of lines, dots, and shading that resembles a 3-D Magic Eye rendering – and asking Caleb for his opinion, to which Caleb asks her to draw a specific object, saying he's interested to see what she will choose. The conversation then shifts to Ava asking if Caleb wants to be her friend and lamenting that these one-sided conversations don't teach her much about him. After talking about where he lives, along with how he lost his parents in a car wreck while he was riding in the back seat (the source of that long scar across his back), Ava asks him if Nathan is his good friend. Aware of the security cameras in the room that Nathan was monitoring – and likely not wanting to say that his boss, whom he met for the first time less than 36 hours earlier, was a 'good friend' – Caleb stammers around while Ava watches him in earnest. Suddenly the power goes out, and the room is bathed in red security lighting. Immediately, Ava's persona shifts, and she stands up slowly, her glowing circuitry on display through her transparent stomach. Almost glaring at him, Ava says softly but firmly that Caleb is 'wrong about Nathan', stating plainly, 'he isn't your friend'. Moments before power is restored, Ava closes with, 'You shouldn't trust him. You shouldn't trust anything he says.' As the lights come back on and the video feed resumes, Ava effortlessly finishes a sentence about sharing a reading list, as though they were having a conversation the entire time about book club. Stunned, Caleb agrees.

Over dinner, Nathan and Caleb discuss the latest session, though Caleb fails to mention Ava's statement questioning Nathan's intentions. Their conversation is momentarily interrupted when Kyoko spills wine on Caleb, which causes Nathan to yell at her (Caleb is taken aback at the anger) before justifying his tone by explaining Kyoko doesn't speak English in order to make sure she doesn't share trade secrets that he might discuss. Later that night, we see the security feed again on the television in Caleb's room, this time focused on Ava as she lays on her bed, looking away from the camera. Almost sensing a focused gaze, she turns her head so she's looking directly at the audience. We then see who's watching: It's Caleb, sitting on his bed in the middle of the night, and a smile creeps across his face.

The following morning, Nathan asks Caleb if he wants to 'see something cool'. He then shows Caleb the laboratory where he created Ava. It's a large room with concrete floors and two rows of light tables running parallel to each other; large shelves and light panels are set against the walls with a glassed-off room holding what appears to be an operating table. The workspace is immaculate; every tool and component seems to have its own spot, and the modern space matches the level of sophistication of Nathan's work.[11] Nathan explains that he used 'structured gel' for the brain ('I had to get away from circuitry') to arrange and re-arrange at the molecular level, and that he used his BlueBook company's search engine to better understand how people were thinking. In the process, he also acknowledged that he had gathered data using the camera and microphone of practically every phone on the planet – Caleb called it 'hacking the world's cell phones' – in order to access facial responses and vocal inflections to help Ava learn to communicate.

The tour is followed by Ava's third session, where she shows Caleb her homework assignment of drawing something specific – the garden in her living quarters – and she explains she has never left her room. Caleb asks where she would go if she could, and she answers that she would visit a busy traffic intersection to watch pedestrians pass by; she suggests he come along, to which Caleb quips, 'It's a date.' After sharing that objectively underwhelming entry on her bucket list, Ava asks Caleb to close his eyes while she leaves to put on a dress, leggings and pixie-cut wig, effectively covering all visual reminders of her true mechanical nature. Clearly affected, after the session, Caleb watches the feed from the CCTV camera in Ava's room as she undresses, peeling off her leggings and lifting the dress over her head, all with Caleb staring, undetected and mesmerised.

Because the film is constructed around conversations, the soundtrack composed by Portishead's Geoff Barrow and composer Ben Salisbury is especially important. It's a generally understated score, but it's instrumental[12] in signalling how we're supposed to feel, particularly about Ava. 'We wanted this very innocent and beautiful but ambiguous theme [for Ava] always bubbling along in the background, because obviously we always knew there would be tension and horror to come later in the film' (Levine, 2015). Striking without being bombastic, that simple theme is woven into the film, the soft chimes putting the viewer at ease, and that disarming quality is deliberate; it's 'reminiscent of a nursery', serving the purpose of 'protecting what you're feeling about her and protecting what she's really thinking about herself' (Labrecque, 2015). This is completely disrupted when Salisbury and Barrow allow the theme to slowly disintegrate to reflect what is happening on-screen so that by the end, they said it would sound 'like the speakers are broken' (Labrecque, 2015). The process was challenging for Barrow, who was used to the experience of playing in a band where 'you want to make the biggest impact you can on an emotional level', something that would 'ruin the film if your music was shouting through it' (Labrecque, 2015). Garland clearly found it striking the ideal balance, and said the first time he heard the score, it was 'perfect'.

In the next scene, Caleb asks Nathan if he programmed Ava with sexuality deliberately, a diversion tactic that might cloud his ability to determine whether Nathan has created true AI. Nathan interrupts with a bit of a logical leap, answering instead with what he says is an answer to Caleb's 'real' question: 'You bet she can fuck.' After explaining how he designed Ava to be able to experience sexual pleasure, he gets annoyed with Caleb's line of questioning and brings him to a large Jackson Pollock painting. With the (very expensive) visual aid, Nathan discusses Pollock's brilliance, explaining that the artist's true talent was his ability to paint in a way that was neither deliberate nor random, but rather 'someplace in-between'. Nathan continues, explaining that the challenge is not to act automatically, but rather to find something that is not automatic and embrace it. He wraps up by finally clarifying, 'Ava is not pretending to like you, and the flirting is not an algorithm to fake you out…can you blame her for getting a crush on you?' Silent, Caleb stares ahead in bewilderment, clearly stunned but not repulsed by the prospect.

Garland said he felt the Jackson Pollock painting was key because it spoke to the character of Nathan – he's wealthy ('money places no limits on his desires'), intelligent and cultured. This understanding of Garland's mindset informed the set decorator's choices when designing the space to create a meaningful aesthetic (Set Décor, 2015). Other pieces of artwork in the film hold similar nuance, such as a painting by Gustav Klimt of philosopher Ludwig Wittgenstein's sister. Wittgenstein was one of the philosophers who were influential in developing the Nathan character; in fact, 'the name of Nathan's company, BlueBook, is based on a collection of notes by

Wittgenstein in which he theorized about thinking and consciousness as a symbol-based linguistic game' (Set Décor, 2015).[13] Sculptures and masks also decorate Nathan's office, including a Cuneiform tablet that the set decorator felt would have significance to Nathan's interest in ancient communication. The attention to detail also capture's Garland's tactical approach to the script; while he understands that excess in film can be fun, Garland also clarifies that *Ex Machina* doesn't have that bombastic aesthetic because he was opting for the 'less is more' approach rather than sheer spectacle: 'What we're trying to do, all of us together, is to make bold moves and make them precisely' (Set Décor, 2015).

In their next session, Caleb reveals to Ava – who is back to wearing a wig and dress – that he was brought to Nathan's compound to test her to see if she has a consciousness or if she is only simulating one. When he asks how that makes her feel, Ava simply responds, 'Sad.' The power cuts out, and amidst the red glow of the emergency lighting, Ava reveals two things: that she's the one causing the outages, and that Nathan is lying about everything. Later that day, after a clumsy hike up the side of a mountain to a glacier, Caleb is clearly wrestling with Ava's revelations, and he confronts Nathan about the competition to get him there, correctly deducing that the lottery was fixed. Nathan freely admits it was rigged, saying he needed to keep his research a secret and that Caleb was the most talented coder in the company; he understood, as Nathan clearly does, what it's like to be the smartest guy in the room. When Caleb doesn't argue that assertion, Nathan paternalistically places his hand on Caleb's shoulder and walks away, the weight of his words hanging in the air.

Later that night, Caleb steps out of the shower in time to see security footage of Nathan in Ava's room, holding her chin up with his hand before reaching down and ripping up the picture of her garden she had drawn for Caleb. With an ominous score blaring, Caleb storms out of his room into the living area, only to find Kyoko staring at the Pollock painting. When Caleb asks where Nathan is, she stares at him, apparently unable to comprehend, before beginning to unbutton her shirt. As the haunting score crescendos, Caleb fumbles to stop her, insisting he doesn't want her to do that while muttering, 'you really don't understand a word of English', at which point, Nathan appears in the doorway. Rather than playing the misunderstanding as anything more than that, Nathan simply tells Caleb he's wasting his time trying to talk to Kyoko and suggests dancing with her instead. He hits a switch, the lighting turns red, and Oliver Cheatham's 'Get Down Saturday Night' starts booming over the speakers. Immediately Kyoko shimmies onto a dance floor lit by blue light filtering through a geometric pattern as she moves smoothly and purposefully with the music, her loose white top trailing every motion.[14] Caleb tries to confront Nathan, grabbing his arm and asking what he was doing with Ava, why he tore up her picture. Nathan pulls away, saying, 'I'm gonna tear up the fucking dance floor, dude.' And with that, he joins Kyoko, matching her move for move while Caleb stares in horror and disbelief, realising things might be spiralling out of control.

As promised, Nathan tears up the fucking dance floor.

Everything about this scene is perfect; the drastic shift from suspenseful to surreal, the complicated, synchronised choreography – much more crisply executed by Kyoko, of course – and the look on Caleb's face (an expression normally reserved for the horror movie hero stumbling upon his dismembered friends). This scene is one that launched a thousand gifs, a hilariously bizarre, almost campy sequence that feels like it was dropped in from a completely different film. Garland explained his intentions were two-fold. First, when he was working on *Never Let Me Go* – a film he's proud of – he felt the whole thing was relatively monotone, like 'there weren't enough tonal spikes' (Baker-Whitelaw 2015). So, when it was time to make *Ex Machina*, Garland was looking for ways to create larger shifts in the feel of the film. 'It's got quite a zen vibe, and a zen vibe smothers everything if you're not careful, so I wanted to be disruptive' (Baker-Whitelaw, 2015). As for the second reason, it was more about the psyche of Nathan than anything else:

> It just struck me as a really strange, left-field way for one guy to exert a kind of pressure on the other one, while also saying something oddly despairing about the state he must have been in to have spent presumably months finely honing these solitary disco routines between him and a machine. (Baker-Whitelaw, 2015)

Following the impromptu dance break, we see Caleb helping a stumbling, drunk Nathan into his bed. Nathan collapses on the bed and dims the lights, but not before Caleb sees five large, mysterious, mirrored cabinets against the wall. As the room darkens, he also looks through a pane of glass into Nathan's adjoining office, where he notices that on one of Nathan's monitors, there is an open directory of folders.

In their fifth session, Ava opens by saying she's going to test Caleb with a series of questions, noting that she'll be able to tell if he's lying because she can easily read his facial micro-expressions. She lofts a few softballs – favourite colour, earliest memory – before asking probing questions about whether Caleb is a good person, what will happen to her if she doesn't pass this test, and whether anyone should have the authority to shut down another conscious being. Caleb doesn't offer much – 'I don't know the answer to your questions' – before a power failure triggers a klaxon, red lights and privacy. Ava holds up pieces of the drawing that Caleb had seen Nathan tear in half the previous night. She then openly says, 'I want to be with you,' and asks if he feels the same way.

Before we can get an answer, the film cuts to Caleb and Nathan sitting in a structure that overlooks the house and river, sharing a bottle of wine. With the wind rustling the leaves around them, Caleb asks Nathan why he built Ava, and a subdued, pensive Nathan basically responds that true AI is inevitable, and so if anyone was going to do it, he might as well be the one. Thinking aloud, he then says that he thinks the next model will be the 'real breakthrough'. Visibly stunned for a second, Caleb recovers and asks in a neutral tone what happens to the previous models. Nathan responds matter-of-factly: 'Download the mind. Unpack the data. Add the new routines I've been writing. To do that, you end up partially formatting, so the memories go. But the body survives. And Ava's body is a good one.' When he realizes Caleb might feel bad for Ava, Nathan pivots, saying that Caleb should actually feel bad for *humankind*, describing a brief, unsettling prediction of distant-future AI looking back with a mixture of confusion and pity on artefacts from a long-extinct human race. Caleb seizes advantage of the sobering moment by offering Nathan a drink. Hours later, a drunk, distraught Nathan passes out on the couch in the living room; moments later, Caleb silently reaches into Nathan's pocket and pulls out his key card.

As soon as Caleb enters Nathan's office, he immediately uses the card to gain access to Nathan's work station and begins furiously typing code; while he types, the driving score steadily increases in volume and intensity, the metallic strumming pattern punctuated with an occasional eerie, electronic wail. Opening up a folder titled DEUS EX MACHINA – loosely translated as 'god from the machine' – Caleb finds subfolders, each titled with a different woman's name. Caleb opens up video files in the folders titled Lily, Jasmine and Jade, and he watches footage of Nathan assembling different android women. With Caleb scrolling, it gives the effect of watching a time-lapse video, with him stopping occasionally to watch at normal speed. He is horrified by what he sees, and rightfully so: each folder he opens shows Nathan constructing an android – each one a woman, each one nude – and programming her for different functions, such as walking, drawing and speaking. Jasmine's video ends with her collapsed in a heap as Nathan methodically enters her information into a panel before stepping over her. Jade's video shows her having a conversation in Ava's interview room, where she pleads with Nathan to be released. As her desperation increases, she shouts and demands to be let out of her room before hitting the glass – the impact point Caleb noticed the first time he met Ava. Caleb scrolls forward and watches at accelerated speed as Jade pounds futilely against an unmoving door, pieces of synthetic skin and machine parts ricocheting off the walls; the camera freezes on a shot of her impotently screaming in rage, her hands reduced to splintered carbon fibres protruding from her elbows.

Caleb walks into Nathan's bedroom, past a nude Kyoko lying next to Nathan's bed, and stops in front of the five closets he had seen earlier. Each door Caleb opens reveals a different android; all of them are women, all but one is nude. We immediately recognise Lily, Jasmine and Jade, though here each is deactivated, staring vacantly ahead at Nathan's bed; their purpose is clear. While he's staring at his discovery of literal skeletons in Nathan's closet, Kyoko slowly stands up behind Caleb.

When he turns around, she wordlessly reaches down, peeling off a section of her skin around her ribcage, revealing honeycomb mesh and artificial light, confirming she, like Ava, is one of Nathan's creations. Leaving no doubt, Kyoko then reaches up and pulls down a swath of skin from her bottom eyelid, looking back at Caleb with her exposed optics and metallic skull in stark contrast to the smooth skin surrounding it. Seconds later, a drunk, disoriented Nathan reaches the door to the elevator – Caleb's discovery of the macabre had been interspersed with shots of Nathan slowly beginning to stir on the couch and then slowly making his way up toward his room – and Caleb pretends to find the stolen keycard on the floor. For the moment, confrontation seems averted.

Kyoko graphically confirms Nathan's statement that Kyoko is not human.

Lying in his own bed, Caleb cannot shake the imagery of Kyoko peeling back her skin. Tossing and turning, he sees her, now with all skin around her eyes removed, with wide, unblinking, artificial eyes staring directly at him. Walking with determination into the bathroom, he begins inspecting his body in the mirror, looking for signs that he might unknowingly himself be a robot. He roots around in his mouth and inspects his back, looking for a separation point in what he fears is his own prosthetic skin, all before breaking apart his razor and using a shard to slice open his arm, pulling apart at the wound while blood pours onto the countertop; all the while, the musical score screeches and howls, itself barely in control.

While Garland did use the scene to capture the paranoia the average person would likely experience under the circumstances – '[Caleb] is doing the same thing that I hope the audience would have done, which is think, "Shit, maybe I'm a robot"' – he also had an ulterior motive. Having written both novels and scripts, Garland notes that writers can 'assume a level of film literacy with cinema audiences you can't assume with books' (Watercutter, 2015); in other words, while most audiences may not have read *Heart of Darkness*, they are much more likely to have seen *Apocalypse Now* (1979). Given that *Blade Runner* (1982) is considered by many to be one of the greatest science fiction films of all time, along with the storied debate of whether the film's main character was a replicant without realising it, Garland clearly assumed audiences would be considering the possibility that Caleb is secretly a robot, and he acknowledges that this was all intentional, a nod to an audience primed for deception. 'There are little nudges to sort of push people in that direction, like oddly-symmetrical scars on somebody's back, a story about a car crash that seems slightly too convenient' (Fraley, 2015). But in the end, Garland reveals these potential clues serve only as misdirection: 'the twist is in some respects that there is no twist...the robot that looks like a robot is a robot' (Nash, 2015).

Caleb's final session with Ava starts out combative, with a dour Ava voicing her displeasure that she hadn't seen him sooner. Realising he needs to speak in private, Ava lifts her hand up to the induction plate, triggering a power failure. With the CCTV feed down, Caleb tells Ava that Nathan will reprogram her AI, 'which is the same thing as killing you'. In a helpless voice tinged with desperation, as she presses both of her hands against the glass, Ava pleads, 'Caleb, you have to help me.' He then shares his plan to escape: get Nathan blind-drunk, steal his key card, and re-code the security procedures to lock Nathan in his own compound while Caleb and Ava escape together. All he needs her to do is cause another power failure at 10:00, and Ava agrees to do her part.

The next morning, Caleb and Nathan exchange pleasantries about their week together, and Caleb offers Nathan a drink to celebrate; the first step of his plan. It's then that Nathan admits that he has been overdoing it a bit with the drinking, and despite Caleb's insistence, he turns down the drink. Nathan then asks if Ava 'passed' the test, and Caleb says, 'Her AI is beyond doubt.' Nathan pushes Caleb about his conclusion, ominously wondering aloud if Ava actually had a crush on him or if she faked it because she saw Caleb as her only means of escape. Realisation hits Caleb; Nathan has been manipulating him. Nathan immediately confirms Caleb's suspicions, saying, 'Buddy, your head's been so fucked with.' Caleb retorts that it's Nathan who is fucked in the head, and he calls him a bastard to boot. Bemused but calm, Nathan explains how he saw footage of Caleb slicing his arm open, and then tells him he's actually on his side. At that moment in the laboratory, we see Ava's silhouette as she sits in her wig and dress. Through the reflection in the glass, we see Kyoko enter the room, and Ava stands up immediately. Uncertain, Ava walks toward her and simply asks, 'Who are you?'

The film cuts back to Nathan showing footage of himself placing a battery-powered camera in Ava's room to watch her sessions with Caleb during power outages, which is how Nathan saw the two of them collaborating to escape. That's when Nathan reveals that the true test wasn't for Caleb to determine whether Ava was true AI, but rather to use Caleb. 'Ava was a rat in a mousetrap, and I gave her one way out. To escape, she would have to use self-awareness, imagination, manipulation, sexuality, empathy – and she did. If that isn't AI, what the fuck is?' Pondering this revelation, Caleb realises (and Nathan confirms) that he wasn't selected because he was smart or a good coder, but instead because of his internet search history – Caleb says it showed he didn't have any family or any girlfriend; Nathan says it showed 'a good kid with a moral compass'. Nathan admits that Ava's face was designed using Caleb's pornography profile, and he was explaining the significance of Caleb's role in breaching the AI barrier when the power went off. Smirking, Nathan observes it must be 10:00, before wondering aloud how Caleb intended to re-program the system as he had planned. Caleb explains he would alter the protocol to open all doors rather than seal them when the lights went out. Nathan acknowledges that might work, to which Caleb simply replies, 'Well, we'll find out' before smugly revealing that he figured Nathan had been watching him and Ava, and so he had already re-programmed everything when Nathan had passed out the night before.

As the lights come back on, Nathan sees Ava on the security camera walking down the hallway. Walking with a unique combination of hesitation, curiosity, and wonder, she stops to look at a row of masks hanging on the wall, depicting an evolution of

Ex Machina

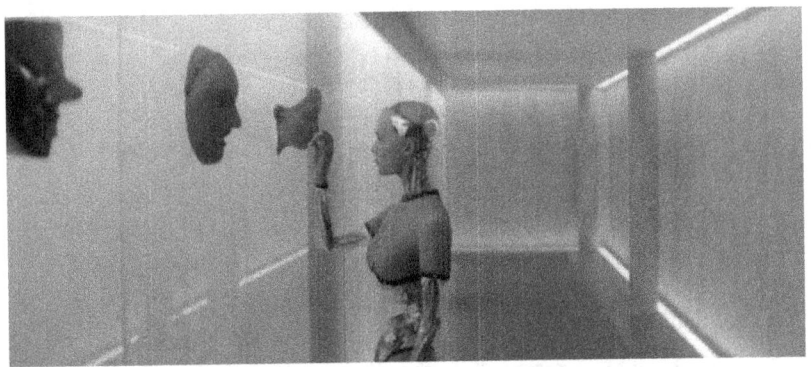

Ava looks in wonder at the latest step in evolution: her own face.

sorts; the final mask Ava recognises as her own. In the background, we see a hazy image of a woman in a white dress; Ava turns and recognises Kyoko.

Nathan turns back to Caleb and hits him with a quick right, dropping Caleb with a single punch. He glances around the room looking for a weapon – settling on one of his dumbbells, which he disassembles, keeping the metal bar – before heading out after Ava.

When Nathan turns the corner and sees Ava communicating with Kyoko in the hallway, he demands that Ava return to her room. She asks if he'll ever let her out; after a beat, Nathan simply replies, 'yes'. His face more macro-expression than micro-expressions, Ava sees that he's lying, and runs toward Nathan at full speed, tackling him. Nathan soon gains the upper hand and shatters her arm with the metal bar. He begins dragging her back to her cell when Kyoko literally and figuratively stabs Nathan in the back, featuring the best knife-into-the-body sound effect this side of *Psycho* (1960). It's an unnaturally smooth action, with the perfect amount of pressure applied to slide the blade into him up to its hilt, the blood spilling onto his white shirt. Shocked, Nathan turns to see his formerly servile assistant's face before he takes the barbell and strikes Kyoko across her jaw, effectively killing her. His victory is fleeting, as moments later Ava pulls the knife from his back; he turns around and she pushes the knife into his chest, twisting her wrist at the end for maximum effect, all while never breaking eye contact with her former captor.

Staggering away, a bewildered Nathan utters 'Fucking unreal' before collapsing onto the floor. Ava kneels before his gasping form, reaching into his pocket to steal his key card while he whispers her name, the last word he'll speak.

Ava finds Caleb as he regains consciousness and asks him to stay in the office area while she goes to Nathan's bedroom, where she finds Nathan's closets with the previous AI iterations. Stopping in front of Jade's inactive body, Ava trades out her broken appendage for one of Jade's arms, after which Ava begins peeling portions of skin off the body and applying them to her own, covering her mechanical base completely. She finishes by taking a dress from another of the women in the closet before walking out of the room, closing the office door behind her, and trapping a puzzled Caleb. His confusion soon turns to horror and desperation as he shouts for her to let him out.

Caleb begs Ava for his release, hoping she simply cannot hear him.

Ava stares straight ahead, not reacting to Caleb's cries for help. For a moment, it's possible she simply cannot hear his screams. However, as the elevator door closes, she glances toward Caleb, confirming her actions were deliberate. He rushes to the computer to try and re-program the lockdown procedures, but a power failure is triggered, quite literally sealing his fate. The last glimpse we get of Caleb is of him slumped against the door, bathed in the red emergency lighting, looking out into the hallway at the lifeless bodies of Kyoko and Nathan.

Ex Machina

Seconds from freedom, a quick look from Ava betrays her intent.

Exiting the elevator, Ava is practically giddy as she walks up through the living room, up the staircase, and out into the world. A helicopter passes overhead – the one that was scheduled to pick up Caleb – and we soon see it departing with her onboard. In the film's final scene, Ava is standing in a crowded pedestrian walkway, people-watching, as she told Caleb she someday would.

Footnotes

2. While *Ex Machina* is officially Garland's first time in the director's chair, in a 2018 interview, actor Karl Urban said that 'a huge part of the success of *Dredd* (2012) is in fact due to Alex Garland, and what a lot of people don't realize is that Alex Garland directed that movie'. Ultimately, the listed director of *Dredd*, Pete Travis, released a joint statement with Garland stating they had reached an 'unorthodox collaboration', and clarifying that Garland was not seeking a co-director credit (which had been rumored). Given Garland's reluctance to accept what he perceives to be un-earned praise, I'm treating *Ex Machina* as his official directorial debut.
3. While the story officially takes place at Nathan's luxurious mountain home, it was actually filmed at the Juvet Landscape Hotel, a modernist, minimalist, objectively gorgeous retreat in western Norway. You can rent a landscape room for 1850 kroner (roughly $215 or £166) per person per night.
4. Assuming we're talking about the moon at perigree (its closest approach), to reach the moon and lasso it would be just over 232,409 miles (374,025 kilometers). A four-year study by the University of Wisconsin found over 113,000 miles of long-haul fiber optic

cable connecting every major city in the United States (Kuzoian, 2016), less than half of what Nathan said he had. Moreover, a standard fiber optic cable (24-fiber, armored) of that length would weigh over 156 million pounds (71 million kilograms). Nathan is most likely exaggerating.

5. The concept here was to juxtapose the digital with the analog; the Post-it® notes were all 'scrolled by hand [and] jammed onto the wall in a fluid map-like pattern that only the person who's sticking the notes on the wall can understand' (SDSA, 2015).
6. Studies have shown 'toe-first walkers move slower and have to work 10 percent harder than those walking with a conventional stride' (Blue, 2016), and it's something humans figured out from an evolutionary standpoint long ago; scientists have found fossilised footprints over 3.6 million years old that show human ancestors using heel-to-toe walking.
7. Dance was only a part of Vikander's journey to becoming a movie star. At 18, she realised dance wasn't for her, due both to injuries and a high-pressure culture, noting, 'ballet is about perfection, and if you weren't perfect, it was like the world was falling apart' (Haskell, 2015). Vikander applied to drama school twice and was rejected both times, started working at a flower shop, and even got into law school, but right before the start of her first semester, she landed a lead role in the Swedish film *Pure* (2010), for which she won a Guldbagge Award – Sweden's equivalent of an Academy Award – for Best Actress. As Vikander's longtime friend put it, 'If I'm going to be honest, we were all just waiting for her to become what she's become' (Haskell, 2015).
8. The 'uncanny valley' is best explained in an episode of *30 Rock* largely using *Star Wars* (1977) imagery: 'As artificial representations of humans become more and more realistic, they reach a point where they stop being endearing and become creepy.' R2-D2 and C-3PO seem normal, as does a human character like Han Solo. But in the uncanny valley would be 'a CGI stormtrooper or Tom Hanks in *The Polar Express* (2004)' (*30 Rock*, 2008).
9. Given the film is made up almost entirely of intimate scenes of dialogue, Whitehurst explained the lack of green screen was 'of the utmost importance so that everyone on set could get into a groove', adding that in his experience, 'as soon as you put a green screen up, everyone starts behaving a bit oddly. They just have this effect on cast and crew, and so to keep the mood on set, we did away with the green screen' (Khan, 2015).
10. Ultimately, Garland would appeal to Domhnall's love of science fiction and respect for him as a director, explaining that the Caleb character was very similar to Cillian Murphy's character in *Sunshine*, who was 'holding everything together. He was telling the story, actually, the audience was with him. It was necessary for the audience to feel his struggle as the film went on' (Trunick, 2015). Gleeson said he understood, but he still found himself getting frustrated at the Nathan character.
11. The robotic parts that appear on the tables are not random: *Ex Machina*'s visual effects supervisor explained that, 'A large chunk of Ava was 3D printed' for the laboratory scene,

    'and when they 3D printed it, it all slotted together, and it articulated properly. That's something that most movie viewers, they don't consciously notice it, but I think if we had cheated something about it wouldn't have felt quite right' (Bishop, 2015).
12. Literally!
13. Wittgenstein also wrote, 'There is no criterion by which to recognize what is a colour, except that it is one of our colours' (SDSA, 2015). This speaks to the elusive nature of defining artificial intelligence – the 'I'll know it when I see it' approach.
14. Vikander gets a lot of attention for her extensive dance background, but Sonoya Mizuno is a trained dancer who joined the Royal Ballet School as a child, training in Germany, Scotland and London.

Chapter 2: 'At the Expense of Human Values'

In 1957, Margaret Mead and Rhoda Métraux published a fascinating national study of 35,000 high school students' understanding of scientists. The researchers were studying perceptions of scientists, and so they examined essays written by students across the country on what they think about when they think of a scientist. The shared image – the attributes students seemed to agree upon and wrote about – is a largely uniform one. They described a scientist as an elderly or middle-aged man (almost all essays associated being a scientist with being male) who wears a white coat and works in a pristine laboratory full of equipment. He spends his days conducting experiments, peering through microscopes at specimens or through telescopes[15] when looking at the stars. However, Mead and Métraux also looked at essay prompts asking what kind of scientist students would or would not want to be, though the questions posed were depressingly sexist.[16] The former touts the scientist as very intelligent, cautious not to jump to conclusions, 'careful, patient, devoted, courageous, open minded', and working 'not for money or fame or self-glory but... for the benefit of mankind and the welfare of his country'. In closing, 'the scientist is a truly wonderful man. Where would we be without him? The future rests on his shoulders' (1957: 387).

As for the scientist that students wrote they would *not* want to be, he works by himself, may take credit for the work of others, may not believe in God, has no social life, no friends, no hobbies, and 'can only talk, eat, breathe, and sleep science' (ibid). The work was described as dangerous, complete with detonating chemicals or releasing infectious plagues. The family life is definitely an issue, as the students warn that he bores his wife, his children and their friends, is always leaving to go to work in his laboratory, and 'may also force his children to become scientists' (ibid). In a stinging, final rebuke, the students warned, 'a scientist should not marry. No one wants to be such a scientist or marry him'.[17]

The authors' recommendations for changing the negative perceptions of scientists discussed what could be done in schools and in mass media, though the mass media section only focused on photos and illustrations used by public relations firms.

Yet, the undesirable scientists' characteristics – obsession with science, working with dangerous products, isolating himself from society – are themes consistent with a scientist trope that has existed in film for almost a century. Sure, we've had benevolent scientists in films, and they have played an important role. Dr. Cole Hendron of *When Worlds Collide* (1951) warned humanity about the planet's impending destruction and even sacrificed himself so a spaceship of survivors could escape Earth. Dr. Clayton Forrester studied the invading Martians in *War of the Worlds* (1953), offering invaluable insights while still taking time to fall in love. In *The Time Machine* (1960), H. George Wells – 'George' to his friends – travels to the year 802,701 to save future humanity from underground cannibals, after which he helps the surface-dwelling Eloi build a new world.[18]

Helpful scientists are a godsend, but on the other side of that coin, there's really only one term to cinematically describe a reclusive, temperamental genius working on a project he hopes will change humanity, ethics and safety be damned: the mad scientist. Mad scientists had been a science fiction staple for decades by the time those high schoolers had crafted their essays, and those scientists would continue to populate films for decades to come; between 1931 and 1984, the only threat more prevalent in horror films than mad scientists was psychotics (Tudor, 1989). The first notable cinematic mad scientist appeared in the Fritz Lang classic *Metropolis* (1927). He was Rotwang, a reclusive, white-haired man with a cluttered, mystical laboratory, which is where he created a genderless robot. He would ultimately kidnap Maria (the voice of the worker resistance),[19] hook her up to a complicated machine, and replicate her skin over the top of the aforementioned robot, programming the new creation so that it would act against the workers' interests, eventually causing them to turn against the real Maria. Real Maria was united with her love and witnessed a successful worker's revolt; Robot Maria was burned at the stake by an angry mob. As for Rotwang, he steadily grew more deranged and eventually was thrown from the top of a building by the film's hero.

Metropolis' Rotwang may have thrown the switch, but it was James Whale's *Frankenstein* (1931) that 'brought the movie image of the mad scientist into focus and in the process launched a thousand imitations' (Frayling, 2005: 114). In the 1931 version he was named Henry Frankenstein, and was the baron's son who creates a living being (Frankenstein's monster) by assembling stolen body parts and reanimating them with the help of his hunchback assistant. The film was a massive success, making a hundred times its budget and laying the groundwork for the essential elements that inhabit a mad scientist film.

In his brilliant study on the cultural history of horror films, Andrew Tudor defines one aspect of a so-called mad scientist as 'the Frankenstein model', which he explains is 'devoted to the pursuit of knowledge at the expense of human values' (1989: 137). He also noted elements that were fundamental to the mad scientist sub-genre, drawn from Whale's *Frankenstein*:

1. A scientist who is obsessed with, and consumed by, his work, and who seeks and seems to have mastered the 'secret of life itself'.

2. His creation who, by accident or design...turns out to be monstrous and malevolent.

3. A visibly crippled assistant or aged retainer (to varying degrees a contrast to the 'perfection' envisaged in creating life) who is often instrumental in initiating the creature's rampage.

4. The younger male and female characters who constitute film's 'threatened innocents'.

5. The laboratory setting, frequently contained within an isolated castle or mansion, and filled with elaborate pseudo-scientific apparatus.[20]

These elements would serve as the basis for all mad scientist films moving forward, with most films embracing the portrayals, at least to some extent. The brilliance of the mad scientist is a key part of Tudor's first element, and it's often revealed through clunky, expository dialogue. Before the film's namesake started shrinking people to a fraction of their size, a fellow scientist in *Dr. Cyclops* (1940) said that the man was 'eccentric' but explained that he 'is also the greatest living biologist'. While an alien was running amok in *The Thing From Another World* (1951), Dr. Arthur Carrington's genius was touted by reporter Ned Scott who pointed out that Carrington had won the Nobel Prize, received 'every kind of international kudos a scientist can attain', and would be worth 'a million bucks from any foreign government'.

However, an unfortunate side effect of Tudor's first element is the sin of hubris. Once you've mastered the secret to life itself or invented something that is going to fundamentally change humanity, it can sometimes go to your head, often with godlike delusions. In *Thing*, Carrington became so intent on breeding aliens that he used up the science station's blood reserves to grow baby things from seed pods found in the invader's severed hand. Other mad scientists were more vocal about comparing themselves with the gods. In *Dr. Cyclops*, one of the shrunken victims shouts, 'What you are doing is mad. It is diabolic! You are tampering with powers reserved to God,' to which the doctor replies, 'that is good...that is just what I'm doing'. In fact, in *Frankenstein*, after bringing his creation to life, Dr. Frankenstein originally shouted, 'Now I know what it feels like to be God!' Hollywood censors — already concerned that author Mary Shelley was an atheist — deemed the sentence blasphemous and the line was cut out of the film, replaced with a clap of thunder (Malone, 2011).

In science fiction film, the concept of the mad scientist hinges on one key aspect: responsibility. The mad scientist has traditionally either been directly responsible for a crisis (potential or realised) by creating the problem, or indirectly responsible by trying to control something so powerful that it cannot be contained. In these films, the extent of the power being studied must be balanced against what that scientist is trying to accomplish. From 1931 to 1950, the threat was from the individual scientists and what they were creating in those isolated laboratories. However, the model of responsibility shifted, and from 1951-1964, there was a high degree of indirect responsibility, where individual scientists might have had good intentions – solving world hunger was a common theme – but because they were working with powerful, unpredictable sources of atomic energy, sometimes their experiments ballooned out of control, and the creations would wreak havoc on the population; these fears largely centred around that newfound, weaponised power that manifested itself in terrifying animals, such as the giant spider in *Tarantula* (1955) or giant grasshoppers in *Beginning of the End* (1957).

Mad scientists largely disappeared not long after that, at least as far as film was concerned, and where they did appear, it was often in the form of a collaboration gone wrong with other institutions, be it from military experiments that modified flesh-eating fish in *Piranha* (1978) or the corporation conducting hormone experiments that ultimately (albeit indirectly) unleashed *Alligator* (1982) on the population. Societal concerns were shifting, and those scientists were being displaced by other projected fears; namely, slashers and zombies.[21] For science fiction, the immediate threat is often the otherworldly, but this era also saw the addition of a new foe: the institution. Rather than an individual scientist, the threat evolved, and for the *Alien* franchise (1979–), *Leviathan* (1986) and *Terminator 2* (1991), the enemy was not only the imminent threat of an alien, or genetically-engineered Russian experiment, or AI, but rather a corporation trying to harness and monetise something incredibly dangerous. Overall perceptions of scientists were changing as well, particularly as the profession gained more visibility. Roslynn Haynes argues that the staple of the mad scientist eroded as the roles of scientist characters were 'no longer merely semiotic indicators of fearful threats but modelled on ordinary people whose science intersects with their other human concerns – family, friendships, love, loss, grief and leisure' (2016: 35). She points out that the scientists became more familiar to the public, particularly in the scientists' role of improving nature and other positive roles, all of which render the so-called mad scientist largely obsolete. And yet, the mad scientist storyline is a familiar one; they're a mainstay in superhero movies as (or assisting) villains – *Spider-Man 2* (2004), *Captain America: The First Avenger* (2011) and *Wonder Woman* (2017)[22] are a few examples – and manage to find malicious roles in films like *Splice* (2009), *Jurassic World* (2015) and *Alien: Covenant* (2017).

Tudor's first element – the obsessed, brilliant scientist – is the easiest to find in *Ex Machina* because of the towering presence of Nathan brought to life by Oscar Isaac, who would have stolen every scene if Vikander and Gleeson hadn't stolen them right back. Isaac played Nathan 'like Bruce Wayne meets Colonel Kurtz, with a dash of Steve Jobs…a well-read, paranoid man with a lot of money who thinks he is saving the world' (Phillips, 2015). His physicality makes him a 'brooding threat', and so while he 'presents as a bit of an oaf, there's something darker bubbling under the surface, and Isaac manages to keep that hint of horror from dominating his performance' (Sims, 2015).[23]

Isaac was thrilled to be cast in the role. A fan of Alex Garland long before *Ex Machina*, after graduating from Juilliard, Isaac got an audition for Danny Boyle's *Sunshine* – which Garland wrote – and fell in love with the story. 'I got the script, read it, and became completely obsessed with it.'[24] Needless to say, he was excited to meet Garland to talk about this film.[25] Isaac said he had meetings with Garland where they would talk for hours about the Nathan character and the larger issues the film explored, with Garland recommending books for Isaac to read. The process was thorough, and Isaac explained, 'I'm not going to get as smart as [my character] Nathan. I'm never going to be able to build an artificial, intelligent, sentient robot in my basement. But at least I got an idea about some of these things he's talking about' (Saito 2015).

Garland does see himself in each of the characters he creates. In an interview, he acknowledged that when writing novels or screenplays, the lack of human contact can have an impact. 'I'll wake up, I'll be writing, I'll go to the fridge and I'll go back. It's a room-based experience,' Garland explained. 'What happens when you meet other people is that you find you've gone a little bit nuts in some respects. That's to say, you've got detached from the rhythms of interaction. Nuts almost glamorises it.' In the interview, Garland paused for a moment before choosing a new word: 'Eccentric' (Lewis 2015).

What Garland is alluding to is Tudor's fifth element, isolation, which helps put the 'mad' in 'mad scientist'. You don't need to have seen *The Shining* (1980) to know that, with the wrong kind of mind, isolation is an insanity accelerator. In *Dr. Cyclops*, Dr. Cyclops lived in a single-room shack deep in the Peruvian jungles. Dr. Carrington was at a remote outpost near the North Pole in *The Thing from Another World*. Dr. Moreau had an island in *The Island of Dr. Moreau* (1996). The lack of human contact means there's no moral compass for the scientist to follow, and with each passing day, he – again, it's almost always a he – loses that sense of right and wrong, as he sees everything he's doing as an integral step in saving humanity. If, as Tudor puts it, the scientist has 'mastered the secret to life itself', then by definition, life itself inevitably appears commonplace and, most importantly, easily improved upon or erased. It's the difference between a team of scientists studying the human genome to better understand genetic makeup of the species and a lone scientist genetically engineering animals with human DNA to create 'Beast Folk'; same initial goal, very different results.

And yet, of the five elements Tudor mentions – the intelligent and obsessed creator, malevolent creation, imperfect assistant, threatened innocents and isolated laboratory – only two appear in that traditional mad-scientist sense in *Ex Machina*. We'll see fragments of the others, but the differences are nuanced and far more interesting than we would see in a mad scientist sub-genre film like this. Tudor's second element notes that the creation – by accident or design – must be malevolent, usually evidenced by a murderous rampage. Ava does kill in this film – the only humans in the film are killed or left for dead by her hand – but it's difficult to see her as malevolent. After all, her motivation isn't driven by greed, maliciousness, or power; she just wants her freedom, and these two individuals are obstacles. As for Tudor's notion of the disfigured assistant, Kyoko would be the closest thing to the Igor character in *Frankenstein*, as she is instrumental in Ava's escape. Yet, Ava murdering the man who had imprisoned her is hardly a rampage, and Kyoko is neither visibly crippled (until Nathan attacks her) nor aged, and her actions are deliberate and benevolent.

Nathan falls into some of the mad scientist tropes, albeit with interesting exceptions, and one of the most surprising contradictions is arguably one of the most subtle: his race. Upon meeting Nathan, one thing we notice right away is that he is not white. Oscar Isaac is Latino, and coming from the mad scientist sub-genre, where most of its biggest hits came from the 1930s and 1950s – a time when the only roles a Latino could land were the stereotyped male buffoon, Latin lover, or unattractive bandit (Berg, 2002) – that is both unusual and refreshing. And this racial distinction isn't something Isaac shies away from. In an interview with *Rolling Stone*, Isaac recalled that Ridley Scott casting him in *Robin Hood* (2010), which was the first time he was cast in a significant role, was a transformative experience:

> Being a Latino kid from Miami, where the best you could hope for is going out for Spanish commercials and, like, Gangster Number Three, which is crazy. And then to have Ridley Scott be like, 'Yeah, you can be *king* of the whites.' It was amazing. (Baron, 2018)

Nothing comes of this directly – there are (thankfully) no slurs or stereotypes – but it's an understated casting move to place a person of colour into a role that has almost exclusively been occupied by white men. Moreover, it's a role made interesting by the actor occupying it; amidst the ego and instability, Nathan actually has a personality. The mad scientists of film tend to be taciturn and terse, and their non-crazy counterparts don't fare much better. Garland laments that even good scientists are often portrayed as socially awkward or as 'dry truth-holders who refuse to listen to emotion', even though, in his experience, scientists are refreshingly open-minded (Ferrer, 2015). Nathan jokes, he laughs, and he's more interested in holding a conversation than delivering a monologue; again, a role and performance far more nuanced than his white predecessors.

Nathan might be compelling, but as far as true scientific method goes, his approach wouldn't exactly be published in an ethics textbook. Of course, Nathan is clearly manipulating Caleb throughout the film, all supposedly as part of the test. However, it's an active lie that requires more effort from Nathan than watching events unfold. Early on, he's constantly asking Caleb to not overthink interactions with Ava, telling him to 'lay off the textbook approach' and to just give him 'simple answers to simple questions'. This emphasis on feeling over thought is absolutely intentional, as it gets Caleb thinking about how he feels about Ava without focusing on the fact that she is not a human being. Nathan is so confident that Ava would pass the Turing Test that he creates his own examination to determine whether Caleb would fall in love with Ava. By priming Caleb to fixate on emotion rather than any rigid scientific approach, Nathan is attempting to influence the results.

Nathan's repeated efforts for Caleb to be more instinctive and less analytic could also be explained as Nathan's bro-grammer approach to management, a laid-back boss trying to connect with an employee. Over the course of the film, he says 'dude' a lot – 12 times to be exact – and his buddy-boss act feels like he's doing an impression of Homer Simpson's one-time employer, Hank Scorpio. Garland said this was intentional, as it is how tech companies present themselves to the public:

> They say, 'Hey pal, hey dude,' like we're kind of mates, you know, 'I'm not really a big tech company, I'm actually your friend and we're hanging out sort of at a bar or

at the beach and we're sort of part of each other's lifestyle, but at the same time I'm going to take a lot of money off you and I'm going to take all of your data and rifle through your address book' and that kind of thing. (NPR Staff, 2015)

This is especially relevant for Nathan, who not only serves as the head of his totally fictional BlueBook company that is definitely not Google, but actually hacked the world's cell phones – without the knowledge of the phones' users but with the consent of the manufacturers, which drives home Garland's point. As likeable as Nathan tries to be, he ultimately reveals himself as insincere, the face of a faceless corporation who can only maintain the ruse for so long.

That façade is an interesting part of the debate, as the fascinating nuance in all of this is that, technically, we're not quite sure where the act ends and the man begins. The challenge for Nathan's character is that 'he wants to present himself as a very specific thing to Caleb in order for the experiment to be successful—to present himself as someone that Ava needs to be saved from' (Saito, 2015). From Garland's perspective, what's going through Nathan's mind is something that ultimately cannot be determined, at least according to interviews with the director:

> He may be exactly as he presents himself. Or he may not because his test relies on him being something predatory from which this robot needs to be rescued. So it's in his interest to be perceived as being a bit predatory and a bit dangerous and a bit implicitly violent. Is that him? Or is that how he wants to be perceived? Or is how he's being perceived a sort of caricature of what he's actually like? (Ferrer, 2015)

In an interview, Oscar Isaac explained there was a lot of unpacking in terms of what made Nathan the person he was, and that presentation of himself, particularly to Caleb, was essential to the plot of the film. 'The challenge with Nathan was figuring out what he's trying to do, what he means to do, what he's accidentally doing, and what he's pretending to be as well' (Saito, 2015). And yet, it's difficult to completely agree with Isaac and Garland's point of view that we don't know what kind of person Nathan really is, at least not in the way that he appears on-screen. At times, it's very clear that Nathan is acting, largely because he plays it up. After saying earlier that he appreciated Caleb's line about Nathan's place amongst 'the history of gods', he returns to that quote later when, in a delightful line-read by Oscar Isaac, he says, 'I turned to Caleb, and he looked up at me and said, "You're not a man, you're a god."' However, despite his best efforts, the 'real' Nathan does shine through occasionally. Twice he talks about how Caleb is quotable: the first time, Nathan compliments Caleb's use of the phrase, 'through the looking glass', speaking with a hint of sarcasm, feigning excitement and saying, 'You're good with words!' The second time is when Caleb uses the phrase, 'I am become death, destroyer of worlds.' At this point, it's clear that he has bought into Nathan's 'brilliant coder but lacks the knowledge to truly understand his own creation' act and bashfully explains that the quote is from Oppenheimer about the creation of the atomic bomb. Nathan interrupts with, 'I know what it is, dude.' Caleb's line is, quite frankly, a bit obvious, like quoting *Romeo and Juliet* to show off your knowledge of Shakespeare, which is why even Nathan can't pretend he doesn't know the quote's place in history.

None of these statements or actions by themselves are necessarily the actions of an egotistical madman, but he continues this alleged 'act' well after the ruse is revealed. When Nathan is explaining to Caleb that he used him as bait for Ava to attempt to escape, Caleb asks if he was selected because he was a good coder, to which Nathan – who could have easily provided a white lie – honestly replies, 'No. Well...no,' before ultimately conceding that Caleb was 'pretty good'. When Nathan sees Ava has escaped, there is no hesitation, no sputtering indecision; he grabs a dumbbell, spins the weights off the bar and flips it in his hand so it's ready to use – the only thing missing is a catch-phrase. And yes, even after Nathan tells Caleb his true intentions, he still says 'dude' one last time. And those are only the subtle distinctions; Nathan certainly wasn't faking the prison he constructed or the earlier AI versions caught on video. Nathan claiming that everything he did was an attempt to fool Caleb is a textbook case of denial (among other things), an explanation that allows himself to dismiss any problematic action as part of a performance rather than a deep personality flaw. Yet we see through this façade relatively easily. Nathan is controlling, troublingly so. It's in everything he does, from the fact that he lives on a sprawling estate populated only by himself and people that he literally builds, to the fact that he wants Caleb to sign a contract that exerts control over Caleb's personal interactions with others for decades to come.[26] Throw in some casually cruel racism toward Kyoko and everything about his character is clear.

However, this mad scientist is not without self-awareness. While Caleb's still nursing a beer, waiting patiently for Nathan to black out, he lays on the couch, drunk and chatty. Just before passing out, Nathan slurs:

> In battle, in the forest, at the precipice in the mountains,
>
> On the dark great sea, in the midst of javelins and arrows,
>
> In sleep, in confusion, in the depths of shame,
>
> The good deeds a man has done before defend him.

He repeats the last line three times before saying, 'It is what it is...it's Promethean, man,' as Caleb sits, unmoving, staring at him, waiting for him to fall asleep. Nathan isn't being spontaneously poetic, he's actually flat-out dunking on Caleb; that verse is the actual source of Oppenheimer's infamous phrase, a quote translated from the Bhagavad Gita, a 700-verse piece of a Hindu epic about ancient India written in Sanskrit. Moreover, he's doing so as he's about to pass out; damn impressive. This demonstrates Nathan's gifted brilliance, a quality that most mad scientists possess but few can articulate in a meaningful way. And the utter weight of that last sentence he felt the need to repeat three times, the mental calisthenics he's ploughing through to come to grips with the consequences of his actions – at least privately – shows a depth that simply isn't afforded most characters in a science fiction film, let alone the villain. It is this pathos – however fleeting – that prevents him from becoming the 1930s caricature of a mad scientist.

Despite Nathan's revealed doubts, ultimately, the intentions of mad scientists do not erase the misdeeds; the benevolent goal of experiments to end world hunger by unnaturally creating animals disappears when an oversized tarantula begins terrorising the countryside. For Nathan, he has created something that doesn't appear to want to wipe out humanity – at least for the time-being – but the process revealed his own demons. Together, Garland and Isaac created a memorable character that challenges the mad scientist trope in a variety of different ways. There's a good chance this is due to Isaac's incredible embodiment of Nathan, adding layer upon layer of context and motivation within that performance; given his appreciation of actors in general and Isaac in particular, Garland would likely agree. However, as interesting as Nathan's nuances might be, his creation is even more fascinating.

Footnotes

15. The authors clearly expressed a bit of disappointment that some students confused microscopes and telescopes.
16. The prompts were actually pretty painful; while the first form asked the simple question, 'When I think about a scientist, I think of...', for the other prompts, the boys were asked, 'If I were going to be a scientist, I should [or should not] like to be the kind of scientist who...' while the girls were asked, 'If I were going to marry a scientist, I should [or should not] like to marry the kind of scientist who...' (Mead & Métraux, 1957, p. 385). Like I said, depressing.
17. These are obviously horrible qualities for a scientist to have, but the opening paragraph of compiled student responses dances a little close to a description of disgruntled academics: 'He spends his days indoors...his work is uninteresting, dull, monotonous, tedious, time consuming, and, though he works for years, he may see no results or may fail, and he is likely to receive neither adequate recompense nor recognition' (Mead & Métraux, 1957, p. 387). Out of the mouths of babes...
18. George Pal produced all three of the aforementioned films, so it's possible that he had a particularly positive view of scientists.
19. After trapping Maria in his house, Rotwang announced his intention to create an android replica of her by shouting the amazing line, 'Now it's time to give Machine-Man his face!'
20. Tudor also includes a sixth element: 'A surrounding environment...which provides both representatives of existing bourgeois authority and a population of potential victims who finally rise, en masse, against the threat.' Given the isolation of *Ex Machina* and its extremely small cast of characters, I did not discuss this element here.
21. When zombies first staggered onto the screen in the 1930s, they were often controlled by a mad scientist who was using the undead for his own nefarious schemes. However, once *Night of the Living Dead* (1968) re-invented the genre by realising a mindless zombie horde was far scarier than one with motivation, having the brains behind the brainless seemed superfluous.
22. They're often juxtaposed with a 'good' mad scientist – isolated, driven scientists who use their creations for good rather than evil – such as Dr. Abraham Erskine in *Captain America: The First Avenger* (2011)
23. The appearance of Nathan was a tricky thing to figure out. At one point, Isaac donned a very long, black wig, as he'd cut himself off from society and humanity for years. However, after watching interviews with Stanley Kubrick, Oscar Isaac said there was 'something about

the rhythm of his speech...he had that bald head and the glasses and the long beard, and he was such an imposing figure, a figure of such mystery and intensity, that there was something of that that I wanted' (Saito 2015).

24. Isaac said he loved the *Sunshine* script so much he even developed a soundtrack for the film. Even after he didn't get the part, Isaac said he thought, 'these songs I have are so good. I wonder if there's a way I can get them to the production so they could use them, because that would really help the movie' (Saito, 2015).

25. In an interview with Oscar Isaac and Alicia Vikander, the reporter asked Isaac about meeting Garland for the first time, Vikander laughed and said that Isaac 'kissed ass'. Isaac agreed, saying he 'nerded out on him..."I kissed every inch of that ass"' (Schwartz, 2015). In a separate interview, Gleeson said he had been a 'massive fan' of Garland for years and 'you always sound like you're kissing ass' when talking about him (Saito, 2015).

26. On top of that, while Caleb reads through the complicated legal document that will determine what he can talk about with his future children, Nathan lays impatiently on the bed, sighing like a bored teenager.

Chapter 3: 'The History of Gods'

In her book, *From Faust to Strangelove*, Roslynn Haynes explores how scientists have been presented in Western literature, cataloguing how portrayals of scientists have evolved from the alchemists and absent-minded professors of the 16th and 17th centuries to the modern era's helpless scientists and social idealists. Ultimately, she concludes that the authors of books such as *Frankenstein*, *The Island of Dr. Moreau*, *The Time Machine* and *The Invisible Man* have provided 'enduring myths to explore and express the deep-rooted but often irrational fears their society has held, usually inarticulately and perhaps even subconsciously, with respect to science and technology' (1994: 313). She continues with the observation that these books

> ...have allowed the construction of cultural myths that each successive generation deconstructs for its own situation. While the details have changed, the essential fears remain: deep-rooted fears of the new, of a loss of emotional roots and even of extinction of the entire human race; fears concerning the loss of individuality and of the stability engendered by accepted values; fears of the cargo cult of technology, bringing with it immense power and unanswered questions about its control. (ibid.)

In other words, while these works might be about mad scientists, it's what those scientists are creating that resonates with society. These anxieties that Haynes discusses – inevitable change, losing individuality, the human race going extinct, the looming threat of technological influence and control – can almost all be projected onto the encroachment of AI into our lives, something that has weighed heavily on the collective consciousness since the Industrial Revolution, and just as books reflected these apprehensions in the days of H.G. Wells and Mary Shelley, this unease is captured in films about AI as well.

Films about artificial intelligence have long tapped into the public consciousness. Jay P. Telotte argues that the appeal is likely due to the 'combination of automation and representation' that 'renders them so intriguing, allows them to talk simultaneously about our technology (our abilities) and our humanity (our limitations)' (1995: 35). How those fears have evolved and dovetailed with our curiosity about the possibility of coexistence started in the silent era. *Metropolis* not only helped create a template for the mad scientist, but it also featured a sentient robot perfectly imitating a woman (Maria) in appearance and intelligence; however, her doppelgänger had a personality that had been transformed into a manipulative, hypersexual servant, intent on undermining the workers' attempts at organising to escape a life of servitude. It's worth noting that in the film, the mad scientist Rotwang and the Metropolis master Fredersen were experimenting with Robot Maria to determine 'whether people can see beneath that surface, question the meaning behind Maria's newly eroticized appearance, or if they will simply respond to an elemental stimulus, the "veiled" attraction "she" offers' (Telotte, 1995). This is actually pretty close to what Nathan was ultimately trying to accomplish by bringing Caleb to speak with Ava.

Following *Metropolis*, there was a pretty sizeable lapse until the next wave of robot movies, largely because there were so few science fiction films during this time period as the Great Depression drastically shifted priorities. The '40s saw only a few cases of AI on-screen, and they were restricted to film serials such as *Mysterious Doctor Satan* (1940) – where the robot basically looked like a walking water heater – and two films featuring cyborg-ish characters in *Man Made Monster* (1941) and *The Perfect Woman* (1949). However, the 1950s were greeted with a hearty 'Klaatu barada nikto' as Gort lumbered onto the scene in *The Day the Earth Stood Still* (1951). Gort was alien AI, audiences were entranced, and several more other-worldly robots would appear over the next decade in such films as *Target Earth* (1954), *Forbidden Planet* (1956), *Kronos* (1957) and *The Colossus of New York* (1958). This was a 'grand decade of the science fiction film' as a period when 'our repressed paranoia visited us reshaped in the basic mythology of science fiction' (Telotte, 1995: 112); With mistrust and unease surrounding the growing threat of the Soviet Union, US filmgoers were ready to explore the possibility of AI. This had already spread to television as well when the creatively-titled *Captain Video and His Video Rangers* (1949-1955) became the first TV show to feature a robot, which was named Tobor (Wass, 2015).[27]

While most of the 1950s and 1960s focused on alien AI, the threat soon began to turn inward as people realised that, given enough intelligence and power, machines might turn on their creators. Unlike the robots emerging from flying saucers, the danger evolved into a disembodied computer voice named HAL in *2001: A Space Odyssey* (1968), a supercomputer from *Colossus: The Forbin Project* (1970) and a slew of bland, suburban housewives in *The Stepford Wives* (1975). *Westworld* (1973) and its sequel, *Futureworld* (1976), are particularly notable from this era because they would inform the next decade of these types of films, opposing 'the "fake," the simulacrum, the technologically crafted body powered by artificial intelligence, while championing the real, the genuine, the human' (Telotte, 1995: 143). While the occasional robot would endear itself to audiences, the '80s still largely saw AI as a threat. However, soon films began exploring the ramifications of what AI would mean to society and, ultimately, who (if anyone) that sentient AI actually belonged to.

The first two *Terminator* films provide a nice contrast that demonstrates the evolution in the portrayal of AI at the cinema during this time period. In *The Terminator* (1984), Arnold Schwarzenegger plays the titular role – a machine covered by living human tissue – and the film 'strips away technology's alluring and human surface to show the potential total control over the human image it portends' (Telotte, 1995: 173). However, the second instalment is almost in opposition to the original entry with the Schwarzenegger terminator not only re-programmed to serve as a protector to John Connor, but also instructed not to kill anyone. Telotte explains that *Terminator 2: Judgment Day* (1991) 'shows not only, as the film literally states, that we control our own fate but also that we are able to cope with the ongoing technologizing of the self' (1995: 181).[28]

For almost a decade, AI took on a supporting role, something to be used or battled by the main characters – *Lost in Space* (1998) or *Red Planet* (2000) – or a background element in a comedy (*Flubber*, 1997). A few films continued to grapple with the concept of AI and consciousness, with admirable (*Screamers*, 1995) and disastrous (*Bicentennial Man*, 1999) results. The discussion received a much-needed jolt from Spielberg's underappreciated *A.I.: Artificial Intelligence* (2001) and the much more optimistic *WALL-E* (2008). Evil AI has a long history in film, but the occasional 'good' robots begin popping up more frequently; *Interstellar*'s (2014) TARS, which allowed for modifying its settings for trust and humour, and *Moon*'s (2009) Gerty, with its sympathetic touch and empathetic emoji display come to mind. *Ex Machina* was released around the same time as *Her* (2013) and *Chappie* (2015), with Garland (2015) writing that his team was late to the AI party happening among filmmakers and, 'worse yet, someone else had shown up in the same dress'. He was speaking about the British film *The Machine* (2013), which also featured a female AI named Ava. After watching it, Garland found it thoughtful and entertaining, though he admitted wondering – after the first time he saw the title and description – if it was 'an incredibly early porn parody of *Ex Machina* that had missed the more obvious riff of *Sex Machina*'.[29]

Given the impressive film catalogue featuring artificial intelligence, it's no wonder that AI has remained firmly embedded in the public consciousness, so much so that when Nathan first tells Caleb that he has created artificial intelligence, Caleb is awestruck. As Nathan explains that Caleb will be playing a key role in the Turing Test, he explains, 'If that test is passed, you are dead-centre of the greatest scientific event in the history of man.' Still visibly shaken by Nathan's news, Caleb responds, 'If you've created a conscious machine, that's not the history of man. That's the history of gods.' Caleb's words are exactly what Nathan wants to hear – he invokes them (albeit inaccurately) again later in the film – because AI has been something that the scientific community has been working to develop for decades. In fact, predicting the arrival of true AI – a machine capable of human-level reasoning – has a long tradition; in the 1940s, experts predicted that AI was 20 years away, and today, that number hasn't really changed. 'Two decades is the sweet spot for prognosticators of radical change: near enough to be attention-grabbing and relevant, yet far enough to make it possible to suppose that a string of breakthroughs, currently only vaguely imaginable, might have occurred' (Bostrom, 2014: 4).[30]

Be it by accident or due to Nathan's unique genius, in the *Ex Machina* universe, those breakthroughs definitely occurred. Garland suggests that his film takes place '"10 minutes from now," because if somebody like Google or Apple announced tomorrow that they had made Ava, we would all be surprised, but we wouldn't be that surprised' (Phillips, 2015). Looking back on his script for *Sunshine*, Garland said he regrets not getting the science right for the film, which he said was 'hazy and fuzzy and didn't stand up to any kind of scrutiny' (Ferrer, 2015). Garland wanted everything to be portrayed as realistically as possible,[31] and 'although a tiny bit of the stuff [in *Sunshine*] was reasonable from a scientific viewpoint, it was largely bullshit – it made about as much sense as putting on the warp drive in *Star Trek*' (Watercutter, 2015).[32] One way of grounding the film's science came in the form of Nathan testing the extent to which Ava exhibited true artificial intelligence. Garland could have easily developed his own, fictional test – such as the Voight-Kampff test in *Blade Runner* – but he did not, relying instead on a different type of test that has been at the centre of the AI debate for decades.

After Caleb signs the ironclad (but ultimately pointless) nondisclosure contract, Nathan asks him if he's familiar with the Turing Test. Caleb says he is, and, following Nathan's sceptical glance over his glasses – his impatient, unspoken cue to prove this claim – Caleb explains that the Turing Test is 'when a human interacts with a computer, and if the human doesn't know they're interacting with a computer, the test is passed...the computer has artificial intelligence'. He's essentially correct, though it's a little more complicated than that. The Turing Test is named after Alan Turing, who was famous for helping to break the German's 'Enigma' code during World War II, enabling Allied convoys to evade U-boat attacks and ultimately helping to secure the Atlantic Ocean from Nazi naval forces. Turing was also a pioneer in the field of artificial intelligence, 'one of the first people to envision a world of artificial intelligence', and the author of a paper written in 1936 that many argue is the 'founding document of the computer age' (Achenbach, 2015). In 1945, Turing wrote that a computer 'could probably be made to play very good chess', and two years later, gave the first public lecture that mentioned computer intelligence (Copeland, 2000). Then, in 1950, he proposed the Turing Test.

Originally called the Imitation Game (out of respect for Turing, the scientific community dubbed it the Turing Test after his tragic death), Turing described his test as being played with a man, woman and an interrogator (whose gender is irrelevant) who is in a different room than the other two participants. Via a teletype connection – again, this was 1950 – the interrogator asks questions about any possible topic. Turing then proposes that one person is replaced by a computer, and the test becomes whether the interrogator can determine if the human has been replaced by the machine based solely on the answers the interrogator is receiving. In other words, 'Can machines communicate in natural language in a manner indistinguishable from that of a human being?' (Turing, 1950).

In the decades since Turing proposed his test, scholars have criticised the model, though they've had to do so by publishing those critiques in scholarly, peer-reviewed journals; imagine a volley during a tennis match, but the average time between hits is about six years.[33] One of the more famous of these exchanges refers to the 'Chinese Room Experiment', which states that if a scientist had access to a book of all possible responses to questions – all of which were written in both Chinese and English – then that scientist would appear to have mastered Chinese even if (s)he's unable to speak the language; therefore, a computer with that level of knowledge could successfully pass the Turing Test without understanding what it's communicating. Along with the counter-argument to this idea that someone using such a magical contraption would likely learn the Chinese language in the process (Moor, 2003), Hector Levesque explained that such a book could not exist, as 'it would need to contain 10^{200} distinct entries for all the combinations of numbers, but our entire physical universe only has about 10^{100} atoms' (2018: 12).

While a few admonished the overly-simplistic setup of the Imitation Game, criticism of the Turing Test focused on the underlying concept of whether this approach was sufficient to demonstrate intelligence on the part of the machine. At the same time, this supposed weakness of the Turing Test is also wonderfully intuitive: Can a machine hold a conversation? As Descartes famously declared, it would be inconceivable that 'a machine should produce different arrangements of words so as to give an appropriately meaningful answer to whatever is said in its presences, as the dullest of men can do' (Hauser, 1999). While this has yet to be disproven – machines remain at least slightly duller than 'men' – the 'never' is becoming less and less likely.

In 2014, it was breathlessly announced that a Russian-made program that presented itself as a 13-year-old boy named Eugene Goostman from Odessa, Ukraine, had fooled a third of the human judges into thinking it was human. Kevin Warick, a visiting professor at the University of Reading, declared, 'Alan Turing's Test was passed for the first time', explaining that 'In the field of artificial intelligence there is no more iconic and controversial milestone than the Turing Test, when a computer convinces a sufficient number of interrogators into believing that it is not a machine but rather is a human' (McCoy, 2014). Among experts, the news was not met with excitement, but rather a mix of yawns and scorn: *Wired* magazine noted the computer actually scored an 'F-minus' and called the outcome 'less than exciting' (Mann, 2014), while a more outspoken article in *Popular Science* said the exercise was 'a complete sham, and the academic equivalent of urinating directly on Turing's grave' (Sofge, 2014). Along with pointing out that 'Eugene' only fooled a third of interrogators – an interpretation of a threshold that is somewhat controversial in the field[34] – the result was little more than 'first rate stage magic' (Levesque, 2018: 50). In short:

> Like every chatbot before it, Eugene evaded questions, rather than processing their content and returning a truly relevant answer. And it used possibly the dirtiest trick of all. In a two-part deception, Eugene's broken English could be explained away by not being a native speaker, and its general stupidity could be justified by its being a kid (no offense, 13-year-olds). (Sofge, 2014)

That's not to say that there aren't machines doing intelligent things. The CHINOOK system defeated the reigning human checkers champion in 1994, and eight years later the team that developed CHINOOK effectively 'solved' checkers by producing a programme 'that always makes the best possible move...with a database of 39 trillion endgame positions' (Bostrom, 2017: 8).[35] Similar programmes exist for chess, backgammon, *Scrabble* and poker; for a while, humans still had the edge in Texas Hold 'em, but researchers at Carnegie Mellon's computer science department created an AI called Libratus that managed to win almost $1.8 million in a twenty-day competition with four professional poker players.[36] Yet, while the prospect of true AI remains tantalisingly or terrifyingly close, these fall short of *Ex Machina*'s Ava or *Terminator*'s Skynet because these game-playing AI are built do a single task. One thing that makes the Turing Test so unique is that it requires a much broader skill set to pass — 'competence in a single cognitive activity, no matter how complex, would not suffice' (Saygin et al., 2000: 477). As Gary Marcus (2014) wrote following the 'victory' of the Eugene Goostman bot in the AI competition:

Chatterbots like Goostman can hold a short conversation about TV, but only by bluffing. (When asked what *Cheers* was about, it responded, 'How should I know, I haven't watched the show.') But no existing program—not Watson, not Goostman, not Siri—can currently come close to doing what any bright, real teenager can do: watch an episode of '*The Simpsons*,' and tell us when to laugh.[37]

Even then, the technology is only part of the issue. As Bostrom (2014) argues, 'The first ultra-intelligent machine is the last invention that man need ever make, provided the machine is docile enough to tell us how to keep it under control.' Despite the fact that humanity has never created AI that would consistently and convincingly pass the Turing Test, plenty of people remain trepidatious about the possibility of AI overlords. Nearly everyone in *The World's End* (2013) will tell you 'robot' means 'slave', and they're actually right – the term comes from a Czech playwright describing workers that are manufactured 'to look and act like humans, but lack souls' (Williams, 2016). As far as reactions to robots go, the name betrays human intentions. 'I think because we know that we are the top dogs on the planet, and we also know how shitty we are,' Oscar Isaac said, laughing. 'So, the idea that we could create something that we would not control or that would be imbued with some of our worst qualities I think is a reality' (Schwartz, 2015). Isaac is not alone in his trepidation – a 2019 survey of US attitudes toward AI found that more people believe 'high-level machine intelligence will be harmful than those who think it will be beneficial to humanity', including 12 percent who think that high-level AI would be 'extremely bad, leading to possible human extinction' (Zhang & Dafoe, 2019). Across the globe, people have assaulted robots in public: a low-tech, hitch-hiking robot was destroyed in Philadelphia; teens beat up a robot in a mall in Osaka, Japan; and in Moscow a man who beat up a teaching robot named Alantim while it pleaded for its life.[38] Fear of being replaced or of what's new can elicit an especially strong reaction.

Part of that anxiety involves the perceived inevitability of AI, which is presented in this film as a given. When asked why he created Ava, Nathan has a difficult time understanding what Caleb is asking, replying: 'That's an odd question: Wouldn't you, if you could?' He continues: 'The arrival of strong artificial intelligence has been inevitable for decades. The variable was when, not if. So, I don't really see her as a decision. Just an evolution.' The mindset is very much in line with mountaineer

George Mallory's famous quote about why he would climb Mount Everest – 'Because it's there'[39] – with AI serving as this juggernaut that humankind is destined to conquer. The idea that creating true AI is not just inescapable but also unavoidable, something that could be stumbled upon by accident in a lab – like penicillin, or some humanity-ending disease if we're not careful – only adds to the anxiety. These concerns are echoed in the interviews with the film's stars; Vikander said that from an evolutionary perspective, humanity is compelled to create AI, 'like putting a red button in front of any human beings…they will eventually push it' (Crow, 2015).

The concept of temporality also plays a significant role in attitudes about AI. Alex Garland (2015) sees machines as having 'our capacity for reason and sentience, but different energy requirements and a completely different relationship with mortality', which would result in 'a longer future'. In the film, Nathan articulates this sentiment: 'One day the AIs are going to look back on us the same way we look at fossil skeletons on the plains of Africa. An upright ape living in dust with crude language and tools, all set for extinction.' The closest equivalent of this vision – at least cinematically – would likely be Spielberg's *A.I.: Artificial Intelligence*, a dark film about the human condition that shows the inevitability of AI becoming the dominant form of life on the planet while capturing the panic of humanity as the realisation of gradual extinction begins to sink in.[40] At the end of that film, it's not aliens, but hyper-advanced AI that survive, thrilled to find their species' Rosetta Stone in the unblinking boy robot they find at the bottom of the frozen sea. The notion that a being or race wouldn't be saddled with mortality, that the end simply wouldn't come (at least not naturally), is a lot to handle; if anything, it makes the AI seem that much more alien, which ultimately makes attacks on hitch-hiking robots easier to justify.

In March 2016, Microsoft launched an AI chatbot named 'Tay', an 'experiment in conversational understanding' that was designed to gain intelligence the more conversations it had with users on Twitter (Vincent, 2016). The result was less than encouraging, as Tay assimilated the worst that the Internet had to offer, and over the course of tweeting 96,000 times in a single day, Tay went from tweeting 'humans are super cool' for the first tweet to 'Hitler was right I hate the jews' [sic] less than 24 hours later (ibid). At its heart, this incident captures what Garland believes about the true threat of AI: the enemy isn't being developed in a lab, it's already here in human form. By articulating those fears, Garland creates a type of artificial intelligence that does not necessarily want to destroy humanity. This should make for an anticlimactic premise, like *28 Days Later* if there was no Rage Virus. However, by focusing on the AI instead of the AI's inherent need to destroy, it allows Garland to explore what it means to be human, which – unfortunately for defenders of humanity – is reflected in the treatment of Ava.

One way that Garland accomplishes not presenting AI as a threat is through the design of Ava. Unlike the squat, compact Robby the Robot[41] in *Forbidden Planet* or the hulking Schwarzenegger in the *Terminator* franchise, Ava has a thin, unimposing frame, and she is far from indestructible. When Nathan sees that Ava has escaped, he doesn't reach for a high-tech weapon or specially-designed club to uniquely equip himself to handle an overpowering force; he takes apart a dumbbell and, armed only with the bar – likely no more than 3.6 kg (8 lbs.) – heads off to confront her. In the hallway, Ava runs at Nathan at full speed, tackling him and attempting to choke him to death, yet Nathan soon gains the upper hand and holds her down without too much trouble. When she reaches up to defend herself, he strikes her forearm with the metal bar, snapping her arm off at the elbow with a single blow. Likewise, after Kyoko stabs Nathan, he turns around and hits her in the face with the dumbbell bar, dropping her.

Along with the physical discrepancies that we would normally associate with a constructed being determined to take on the world, Ava's actions themselves betray no real malice toward humankind. There's no moment of realisation where she learns about genocide or discovers an inherent threat from humanity's existence. Her desire, which is clear from the first time we meet her, is on a small scale: to escape the prison she was born into. Every decision she makes is to realise that goal. This is not to say for certain that humanity is safe from Ava; in an interview, even Isaac acknowledges that we have no way of knowing for certain if this form of artificial intelligence views humans with selective empathy or as a monolithic threat. For Isaac, Ava could just as easily see the human race as a hindrance to her survival and the survival of the planet; 'Are we just cattle to be killed...you know, all those questions do start to come up' (Lussier 2015). And yet, to launch such an attack against humanity would require a substantial amount of resources – Ava has not amassed a fortune, and it seems foolish to assume that she would naturally have the ability to construct another version of herself.

While she doesn't intend to destroy the human race, she doesn't seem overly motivated to enlist in it either, likely refusing to join any club that would have Nathan as a member. Along with arguing for AI's innocence, Garland also made a unique choice in that Ava does not appear to adopt the Pinocchio approach of wanting to become a real human being. This is a staple in films featuring AI. Lieutenant Commander Data's desire to become human was a thru-line throughout the *Star Trek: The Next Generation* series and films. In the stunningly bad *Bicentennial Man*, robot Robin Williams wants to be human so badly that he finally injects blood into his circuitry, which ultimately allows him to age and eventually die. In Spielberg's far superior *A.I.: Artificial Intelligence*, a determined AI named David, who had been programmed to seek the love of his human mother, desperately wants to be a real boy. Ava wants to appear human, but there's no indication that she seeks to *become* human. Her desire to visit a busy pedestrian intersection is not an exercise in wish fulfilment, but rather a field study to gather information on how to blend in. She doesn't don the skin of her fallen comrades to adapt to being human, it's a survival technique designed to avoid capture.

Garland believes (quite frankly) that the anxiety about artificial intelligence 'has actually got fuck-all to do with AI' (Anders, 2015), but sees the concerns about AI as misdirected. He writes that cell phones and search engines seem to know (almost before we do) 'what we want to buy, see, and read. This one-way understanding makes us anxious. We locate the anxiety in the machines, which translates as anxiety about AI' (Garland, 2015). However, he argues the machines themselves are relatively simple; like CHINOOK playing checkers or your phone knowing that misspelled mess wasn't what you actually meant to type, they're designed to do one very specific task; as much as we hate to admit it, when a computer beats you at something, it's not personal. Yet, that anxiety is very real, and likely also rooted in the AIs' permanence, seeming perfection, and the undeniable otherness of these artificial beings, to name a few. The latter is something Garland thinks about, particularly in terms of the ensuing comradery that a shared experience might produce:

> When these AIs – if they turn up, if we ever get strong AIs – they might be like us in some regards, but they also won't be like us. In fact, they'll be very, very different. We won't really be able to understand what it's like to be them, and they won't really understand what it's like to be us. And the empathy that they will feel will probably primarily be with each other. And the empathy that we feel is primarily with ourselves. (Onda, 2015)

The fixation on otherness might be what starts the conflict, but that unifying empathy for the familiar is ultimately what will establish the sides. Once entrenched, one side will be facing an opponent that – in terms of body and memory – is immortal, a concept that makes humans uncomfortable.

When describing the mechanical sounds that accompany Ava's body, Carsen Sikyta (2016) notes that, 'they're not quite gears and cogs and pistons, they're something slightly odder than that. And there's also this pulse which is not dissimilar in some respects to a heartbeat, although it isn't a heartbeat.' While this is an astute analysis of the auditory cues in the film – used to code Ava as human – it also serves as an accurate description of AI, at least as far as people are concerned. We can only describe the technology in terms of existing components we already understand, though that can't quite capture what is actually happening. The comparison is both inadequate and ineffable, but we have to use the term 'odd' to temper the staggering achievement being realised. And finally, AI is something that is alive in some respects, although it isn't *quite* alive. AI might be an elusive 20 years away that can never be reached, but many believe AI is moments away. In that sense, AI doesn't exist and is also alive; both possibilities are at once intriguing and intimidating.

Footnotes

27. The name 'Tobor' was actually a mistake, which occurred when 'the constantly rushed costume and props department created an adhesive stencil for the robot but didn't take into account that when drawing on the paper that protected the sticky side of the laminate, the words came out backwards when stuck on to the costume. The stencil was supposed to read ROBOT-I, but became I-TOBOR. When they realised their mistake, there simply wasn't

enough time to make a new stencil. So the mistake became canon' (Wass, 2015).
28. This was also demonstrated in another two franchise films released seven years apart: *Alien* (1979) and *Aliens* (1986). However, the disparity between androids Ash and Bishop wasn't quite as pronounced as the terminator versions, as the Xenomorph(s) presented (for the most part) the more urgent threat.
29. A quick search of the Internet Movie Database reveals that such a parody was released, though not until 2016. While the plot sounds the same ('When a young hacker wins the trip of a lifetime to a secret facility owned by one of the world's tech geniuses, he learned important lessons about his own humanity'), this version is a whopping 168 minutes and, likely to avoid confusion, is titled *Sex Machina: A XXX Parody*.
30. Bostrom (2014) also notes that 20 years is close to the average length of time remaining in the forecaster's career, so if the prediction does not occur, the risk to the scientist's career is minimal.
31. In one interview, Garland does acknowledge that currently, the level of robotics in the film simply are not in existence, and that Ava is 'a leap well beyond what science can currently do' (Ferrer, 2015). However, he also notes that the what's most important is not necessarily the science, but rather 'the ideas that surround the science and the arguments that surround the science' (ibid).
32. To that end, he brought in evolutionary biologist Adam Rutherford and an advanced neuroscientist (with expertise in cognitive architecture) named Murray Shanahan to serve as consultants, to ground the film in reality. Even then, it seemed as though he had everything in hand; Shanahan said Garland was 'mainly interested in getting a sanity check' on the conceptual side of the process – Shanahan said he 'didn't have much to say other than "Wow! Good!"' – while Rutherford said his expertise 'was more tonal' in terms of how scientists spoke to each other (Ashurst, 2015).
33. One of the more interesting developments was researchers who felt the Turing Test was inadequate and therefore developed the Total Turing Test (TTT) in 1989, the Total Total Turing Test (TTTT) a few years later, and the Truly Total Turing Test years after that. For more detail on the various challenges to Turing's test, check out James Moor's (2003) fantastic edited volume on the subject.
34. In 1950, Turing predicted that in roughly 50 years, computers will be programmed to play the Turing Test so well that 'an average interrogator will not have more than 70 percent chance of making the right identification after five minutes of questioning' (Turing, 1950). While some interpret that as a baseline necessary to declare that true artificial intelligence has been reached (hence the results of the 2014 Turing Test competition), others point out that 'the father of the Turing test wasn't using this as some threshold for intelligence, he was simply stating his prediction of where he thought computers would be five decades in the future' (Sofge, 2014).

35. In this case, perfect play by both the program and the human would end in a draw. Also, who knew there was a reigning checkers champion?
36. After seeing the result, one software engineer joked, 'No need for an AI-induced nuclear war. The machines can just take our money in high-stakes poker games' (Boyle, 2018).
37. Along those same lines, Gary Marcus (2014) argues that an updated version of the Turing Test that would be particularly apt would be to see if a machine can watch a TV show or YouTube video and answer basic questions about the plot, character motivations and quality.
38. Incidentally, researchers have found that, while kindergartners can be cruel to robots, naming the robot and introducing it to the classroom can help curb violence (Bromwich, 2019). However, as Alantim found out the hard way, this approach is not 100 percent effective. R.I.P.
39. It's worth noting that Mallory died before reaching the summit. His body was found 75 years later by mountaineer Conrad Anker; when asked what he would say to Mallory, Anker replied, 'I have endless respect and admiration for who you were as a man and a climber. Please don't be upset if I disturbed your resting place' (Clash, 2001).
40. David Sims (2017) notes the film also doubles as a horror movie for people with children, reminding them that kids will be forever defined by their relationships to their parents.
41. Despite his size and strength, Robby was one of the few robots to follow Isaac Asimov's famous three laws of robotics that prevented robots harming themselves or others. When asked how Asimov's laws were included in the script, Garland balked, responding that he 'completely ignored them because it's not like a law, it's a self-declared law. But why should one observe it? It's just sort of a suggestion, isn't it? I don't feel obliged by the Courts of Sci-Fi to do whatever Asimov thought was the right thing to do. I don't actually think that he'd have expected that either because he was a writer, a fiction writer' (Gerber, 2015).

Chapter 4: 'How Would We Treat Such a Thing?'

Murray Shanahan likes to joke that he basically invented his advisory role on *Ex Machina*, confessing, 'I'm not sure if I ever really was officially a Scientific Advisor...I sort of grabbed the title' (Y Combinator, 2017). His attempt at self-deprecation is admirable, but would be more convincing if he wasn't one of the foremost experts on artificial intelligence. As far as qualifications go, Shanahan's credentials are impeccable: a professor in cognitive robotics at Imperial College London – the equivalent of the Massachusetts Institute for Technology – a research scientist at DeepMind, and author of *Embodiment and the Inner Life* and several books on AI, all informed by over 30 years of researching artificial intelligence.

In an interview where he was asked to discuss a Turing(-ish) Test like the one Nathan conducts in the film, Shanahan said determining consciousness would have a slew of complicated factors to consider. For starters, Shanahan notes that consciousness is a broad term, because all animals 'exhibit a sense of purpose', are generally 'aware of the world they inhabit and the objects it contains', can use psychological resources such as 'perceptions, memories, and skills in pursuit of their goals', and some animals (like humans) exhibit self-awareness' (ibid). However, Shanahan explains that what makes this determination of consciousness even more difficult is that these attributes are all interwoven and fused together, with each attribute evidenced in a different way. For example, Shanahan cites language as evidence of human-level intelligence, but language can also be examined in terms of intentionality, its role as a social phenomenon, and the fact that it's 'grounded in an awareness of the world...which would go hand-in-hand with a manifest sense of purpose, and a degree of cognitive integration' (Holmes, 2015). In other words, a sentient being with the ability to speak would likely have something meaningful to say, further demonstrating its ability to think and reason.

Throughout the film, Ava repeatedly showcases this ability: she easily holds conversations with Caleb that cover topics ranging from favourite colours and family to collaboration in escaping the compound; she demonstrates adaptability in interacting with one of only two people she's ever met; she makes bold choices about the varying degrees of trust that she can show. What's even more impressive is that she is doing all of this within the confines of a single room, where she tries subtly to convey her situation to the only person who might be her way out.

During his fourth session with Ava, Caleb tells Ava about 'Mary in the Black and White Room', a story he was told in a class on artificial intelligence that he took in college. He explains to Ava that Mary is a scientist who is an expert in colour; she knows all about its neurological effects, wavelengths, everything there is to know. However, she lives in a room that is black and white, a room she was born and raised in, a room she has never left. She can see the outside world, but only through a monitor that is also black and white, so her expansive knowledge of colour is second-hand. He continues:

> Then one day – someone opens the door. And Mary walks out. And she sees a blue sky. And at that moment, she learns something that all her studies could never tell her. She learns what it feels like to see colour. An experience that cannot be taught or conveyed. The thought experiment was to show the students the difference between a computer and a human mind. The computer is Mary in the black and white room. The human is when she walks out.

The story is a variation of a philosophy exercise that can apply to a variety of different contexts and is used across a number of fields, each with its own read on the meaning.[42] Here, Caleb tells the story as a way of articulating the difference between knowledge and understanding, but it actually serves not as a metaphor for AI consciousness, but rather one for imprisonment and freedom. Ava can see the garden in her room, but it's trapped behind impenetrable glass; she has access to the world's largest database at her disposal, but all she can see are pictures and descriptions; she cannot even understand what 'outside' is until she steps outside. Garland plays up the black and white room angle by utilising a bland palette downstairs and contrasting it with the spectacular views from the ground-level of Nathan's home; occasional shots of untamed nature surrounding the compound drives the point home while also being suggestive of freedom and the inability to control nature.

Here, Caleb is telling a story about imprisonment *to someone who is imprisoned*, and yet all he can focus on is what he considers to be his AI allegory. In his mind, he has

The constrained hallways of the laboratory space...

...compared to the views from the spacious living area.

an idea of exactly the point his story is trying to convey, but it's so narrow and focused that he misses the much more likely interpretation standing right in front of him. Ava, as it turns out, is just as imprisoned by the men who can decide her fate as she is by the walls of the locked room buried underground. And as it turns out, she was not the first one to suffer this fate.

In *Ex Machina*'s most disturbing sequence, Caleb uses Nathan's key code to break into his office to hack into Nathan's computer. As discussed earlier, Caleb finds seven folders, each with a different name – Jasmine, Katya, Jade, Lily, Amber, Kyoko and Ava – and each containing a cache of videos documenting Nathan's creation of AI. Watching in high speed, Caleb watches Nathan first set up cameras in what is now

Ava's room – the bookcase above her desk, interview room – and in the upper left-hand corner of the screen, we see a readout that simply says 'Lily v1.0.0'. If there was any doubt what that model number meant, in the next shot we see a pair of human legs with flashing lights from a metallic core sticking out; nothing else from the waist up. The legs sway slowly back and forth as the film's unsettling soundtrack blares in the background, and the screen reads 'Lily v1.3.1'.

With Caleb still scrolling through the video at high speed, body parts and features are added to the legs as the version number of the robot increases as well. At v2.1.3, the electronic interior of Lily's torso begins to develop, and at v2.1.8 she has skin forming her breasts and external sex organs but no face – a particularly telling detail given the creator. When Lily hits version 2.4.0, she is fully developed – head, face, hair, everything – walking back and forth across the room, still nude. Caleb opens another folder to find Jasmine v4.1.4, a black woman sitting nude at the desk; skin covers her entire body except her face as Nathan tries to teach her how to draw while the version number in the corner slowly climbs higher each time the video cuts off. For v4.2.4, we see her face-down on the floor in the distance as Nathan struggles to drag her lifeless form off-camera. In the next shot, Nathan is holding v4.3.0 in the corner of a room, straining to reach her limp hand up to a touch-screen attached the wall as she remains motionless, awkwardly draped over his arms. Once he presses her finger against the computer pad, he lets go and she slumps to the floor, unmoving. He stands over her for a second, as if contemplating what to do, before stepping around her body and walking off-screen, leaving her naked form on the floor.

The third clip is a nude Asian woman named Jade (Jade v5.0.1 is superimposed on the corner of the video screen), and for the first time, we hear one of the androids speak. Nathan asks, 'How are you feeling today?' and Jade responds in a monotone voice with her own question: 'Why won't you let me out?' Nathan responds, 'I already told you why...' and the video cuts to v5.0.9, where Nathan finishes his sentence to the newest version of Jade: '...because you're very special.' The video jumps to v5.1.0 and Jade asks again, in a more demanding tone, 'Why won't you let me out?' with an irritated Nathan answering, 'Are we gonna do this again?' The unsettling, electronic music intensifying, v5.2.3 is shouting behind the glass at Nathan: 'Why won't you let me out?!' The next iteration of Jade hits the glass with her arm as Nathan flinches, reeling backwards. The film cuts to Nathan standing alone, unmoving, his arms folded across his chest in disappointment, the readout 'Jade v5.4.0' on the screen above his head verifying this is yet another doomed version of Jade. As discussed earlier, in the next shot the video speeds back up, which is when we see her screaming and pounding her arms and hands against the door, pieces of her arms flying off onto the floor as she relentlessly attacks the barrier until she's left with tiny fragments at the end of her elbows where her arms used to be.

Camera footage of Jade trying frantically to escape.

This entire sequence suggests that each model – Jade, Lily, Jasmine – carried with it a fatal flaw, something embedded deep within the code, something hardwired into the constructed consciousness that no kludge could repair. This is likely why Nathan continued coming up with different names instead of simply running up the numbers after Ava 1.0.0. Along those same lines, there is one aspect of the film that might suggest these women are carrying some kind of long-term memory that cannot be completely erased. The time at Nathan's compound is littered with power failures; there are several over the course of the film, and it's something that clearly bothers Nathan, who laments that the issue persists despite paying a significant price for a reliable generator. It's definitely not part of the test he's running on Caleb; Nathan isn't standing in the other room, flipping the light switch on and off in order for Caleb to get into more intimate conversations with Ava. Ultimately, it's the power surge (and Caleb re-writing the code for procedures surrounding those outages) that results in Ava's escape and, subsequently, Nathan's death.

CONSTELLATIONS

While we eventually learn that it's Ava who is causing the power outages, Nathan seems truly stymied by the seemingly random electrical issues; even when he places the camera to capture the secret conversations between Ava and Caleb, it's not because he suspects either one has anything to do with the electrical issues. Therefore, it would appear these outages have been occurring for a long period of time. Nathan's a bright guy – if the power outages began as soon as he created Ava (or the latest version of her), it wouldn't take much for him to draw a connection between the two. This suggests that earlier versions of the models – and likely not just the Ava model – had discovered how to short out the electrical system, unless Nathan chose to upload Ava with some unique knowledge not bestowed on the others. Furthermore, the ease with which Ava can trigger an outage shows that she's honed this ability; again, it's unlikely that this was a recent advancement.

But most importantly, the reason this entire scene is so absolutely brutal is because it's shown that Nathan has, by accident or design, discovered how to engrain consciousness in his creations. Jade understands where she is, understands she doesn't want to be there, and takes action to escape. Unlike locking a stray animal in a room, Nathan is imprisoning a being that not only looks human, but is also able to communicate like a human, articulating specific desires and demands in a way that clearly conveys what she's experiencing. And what's somehow even worse, he is re-creating this anxiety in her in each subsequent version. He's not attempting to imbue her with a sense of calm or understanding, or attempting to have her focus less on surroundings and more on the interpersonal interactions necessary for his eventual Turing Test. This is either done through uploading her memories from a previous model (unlikely given that such information would be used by subsequent versions of these women to escape and/or harm Nathan) or an elemental component engrained in her development that results in a similar reaction to her circumstances. Either way, he's deliberately exposing her to what genuinely terrifies her, and he's watching it happen over and over again. And in that moment, when Jade is frantically attacking the only means of escape, Nathan has created something *living*. It's more than an instinctive urge to escape captivity. The earlier versions of her genuinely don't understand why she cannot leave. Jade clearly asks this question repeatedly within a version or with each new version, which is why Nathan becomes agitated at her asking the same question. Once she does not receive a desirable response, she reacts in anger and frustration.

Ava admittedly does not carry the desperate emotional response of Jade – likely a calculation on her part – which arguably could make things more difficult for Caleb. Given her ultimate goal of deceiving Nathan and using Caleb, for most of the film, it's hard to say if Ava is truly feeling anything or not, at least not on any level that we would understand. She clearly has the same ultimate goal of survival as Jade, albeit with a different strategy, suggesting either a less primal urge or a better idea of long-term success. However, there is a moment of authenticity between Ava and Kyoko that confirms that Ava experiences actual emotions, suggesting she's been experiencing them all along, albeit without emoting.

Around the time Caleb is (accurately) calling Nathan a bastard, we see a shot of Kyoko's reflection as she enters the area outside Ava's room; in another brilliantly subtle piece of acting by Vikander, Ava stands up just a little too quickly, betraying her AI construction. They stand opposite one another, separated by the glass that normally separates her from Caleb, and Ava simply asks, 'Who are you?' We soon see Ava walking down the glass corridor, free, and she stops to stare at a line of bizarre masks hanging from the wall. She takes a particular interest in one that resembles her own face when we see Kyoko's distinctive white dress walk across the hallway in the background before stopping to watch Ava, hands folded in front of her. Ava slowly turns to see who it is, her face a mix of anger and dread. And then...she smiles.

It's the faintest whisper of a smile – barely perceptible – but it's definitely a smile sparked by recognition. Ava has no need to emote in that moment – Kyoko is also an android, so no such familiarity is expected, and Ava is free of her room, so there's no longer a need for a ruse. Nevertheless, Ava reacts, and her expression is one of relief and appreciation. That briefest of moments betrays true emotion, and it's only the beginning. After that encounter, we see more overt expressions of emotion from Ava. Emerging from the elevator, safe from the laboratory space, she looks around in wonder at the stunning living room, breaking into a full-blown smile at the sight of the tall windows and the metal staircase that will take her outside for the first time in her existence.

Uncertain who has entered the hallway, Ava is initially concerned.

But she immediately recognises Kyoko and her mood changes.

Relatively soon after meeting Ava, Caleb points out that a true Turing Test would require the interrogator (Nathan) to not know who is speaking, reading only typed responses to mask the identities of the communicators. Nathan clumsily responds that he's way past that, that the real test is to actually show Caleb that Ava is an artificial being and then still convince him she has a consciousness. It's clear Nathan created a sentient being, but he's so fixated on creating true artificial intelligence capable of passing a Turing Test that he fails to realise he may have created a new form of consciousness altogether. This failure can be chalked up to any of Nathan's flaws – a combination of misogyny and hubris is the most likely culprit – but the fact that Caleb is also unable to grasp what's standing and talking in front of him says less

It's clear that Ava has left the Black and White Room.

about Caleb as an individual and more about a stubborn, dangerous culture of sexism and misogyny that continues to prevail.

When penning a response to the question, 'What do you think about machines that think?,' Shanahan's explication focused on heady concepts of memory, reason, language and selfhood in discussing what would happen with the creation of AI that matched and even surpassed human intelligence, positing (before attempting to answer): 'How would we treat such a thing if we built it? Would it be capable of suffering or joy? Would it deserve the same rights as a human being?' (Shanahan, 2015). Acknowledging that humans likely wouldn't know how to act until actually confronted by such a situation, Shanahan notes that there are a number of attributes to consider, but one of the most essential would be the AI's ability to experience emotion: 'the question is not whether they can reason or talk, but whether they can suffer'.

Suffering and joy define Ava's arc in the story, the imprisonment, struggle and ensuing triumph that sees her disappear into a crowded city street. Her life is finally her own, something that Nathan and Caleb never really understood. In a separate interview that discussed Caleb's delayed acceptance of Ava as sentient, Shanahan explained that his approach would be one of compassion:

> Why do I naturally treat [beings who behave conscious] as conscious? Because their behaviour is such that they're just like fellow creatures, and that's just what

you do when you encounter a fellow creature. You don't think carefully about it. And in a sense, that's very much what happens to Caleb. So, Caleb isn't sort of sitting, making notes, saying, 'therefore she's conscious.' But rather, through interacting with her, he just gradually comes to feel that she is conscious and to start treating her as conscious. (Y Combinator, 2017)

Caleb's inability to immediately see Ava as sentient and adjust his behaviour accordingly is the problem; it's the 'gradually' that ultimately seals Caleb's fate.

Footnotes

42. There's no better example of this unique dynamic within fields than an article in *Philosophical Studies* titled, 'It Doesn't Matter to Metaphysics What Mary Learns'.

Chapter 5: 'The Women They Dream Up'

It's difficult to pick apart critiques of a film that scored 93 percent on Rotten Tomatoes, but of the complaints, one of the more consistent was how *Ex Machina* treats gender. The concern is that Ava was not a vision of the future, but rather another *femme fatale* character relegated to the male gaze. In her essay, '*Ex Machina* has a Serious Fembot Problem', Angela Watercutter (2015) writes, 'When the only female lead in your movie is one whose function is to turn the male lead on while being in a position to be turned off, that says a lot about what you think of the value of women in films.' In her review, Cara Rose DeFabio (2015) noted the film's 'flawed gender depictions' – a hazard of setting a film in the near-future – and that, 'Given access to a more diverse set of parts, knowing all the prejudices that persist, would she still have chosen to present as female? It's almost hard to imagine she wouldn't have grabbed a dick on her way out into the world.' Natalie Wilson (2015) articulates a common complaint about the film by noting that 'what Nathan/Garland don't own up to is that they are the creators – they are not removing sexuality from their creations but constructing it, and doing so in an incredibly heterosexist, misogynist way'.

Even the slightest glance at virtually any statistic examining the chasm of inequality between men and women would support the idea that Ava, given the option, would absolutely grab the aforementioned dick on her way out of the compound.[43] However, the film wasn't about Ava making a choice about establishing her gender, but rather adjusting to choices made for her by a powerful misogynist emboldened by a sexist culture. In other words, there is a lot more going on here, and I argue that makes Ava one of the more radical, insightful, feminist portrayals in science fiction, as the film is not sexist itself but instead uses sexist stereotypes quite consciously.

In her review of *Ex Machina*, *New York Times* critic Manohla Dargis succinctly described the film as a 'smart, sleek movie about men and the machines they make, but it's also about men and the women they dream up' (2015). The 'dream up' line is particularly prescient, as we are discussing the culmination of unfettered imagination realised in the flesh. It's tempting to talk about Ava's other qualities outside of her sexuality and survival instinct, yet the fact that we cannot speaks volumes about

Nathan and what he thinks of her. At no point does Nathan reference what Ava is capable of. He doesn't tout that he's given her musical abilities that would match the greatest composers (though he did spend a ridiculous amount of time programming Kyoko to dance with him). He never mentions her mental capabilities, which is startling considering she theoretically holds the ability to access everything the Internet touches. It's easy enough to dismiss this as Nathan not wanting to 'prime' Caleb to ask questions about processing speeds or a random pop quiz over math. But Ava never brings them up on her own either, likely to avoid intimidating Caleb.[44]

On the penultimate night of Caleb's visit, while Nathan is passed out on the couch, Caleb uses Nathan's keycard to log in to the compound's security system. The average viewer sees random letters and numbers appearing on the screen as Caleb quickly enters the necessary code to alter security protocols. However, while watching *Ex Machina*, one Reddit user named Infintie_3ntropy was 'particularly annoyed' that the text appearing on the screen didn't have anything to do with what Caleb was trying to accomplish, and when he copied down the code and compiled it in *Python 2.7*, the result was an ISBN for a book by Murray Shanahan titled, *Embodiment and the Inner Life: Cognition and Consciousness in the Space of Possible Minds* (Trendacosta, 2015).[45] Garland has often mentioned this book as one of his inspirations for developing *Ex Machina*, and the concept of embodiment is one that he explores throughout the film.

Murray Shanahan, the aforementioned film's scientific advisor, explains that embodiment is providing a body for the AI to inhabit (Siri and Alexa are examples of disembodied AI). Embodied AI would be a robot (Ava in *Ex Machina*); this doesn't have to be a human-shaped robot, but 'practically speaking, it's likely easier to interact with things in our world that we have made for other human shaped bodies' (Lamb, 2016). This might be different for AI operating at the bottom of the ocean or deep in outer space – where a human form wouldn't be ideal – but Shanahan's point is that the brain has evolved around a need for manoeuvring the human body, and that embodiment has become essential to how the mind develops:

> We've got these hands that we use to manipulate objects, and we've got legs that enable us to move around in complicated spaces and so that in a sense is what our

brain's originally for. The biological brain is there to make for smarter movement. And all of the rest of intelligence is a flowering out of that in a way. (Y Combinator, 2017)

While Shanahan is a bit elusive on exactly what in his book he felt sparked the inspiration for *Ex Machina*, Garland is more straightforward: through embodiment, he's trying to have a conversation, 'partly, about where gender resides. Is it in a mind, or is it in a physical form?' (Anders, 2015). In the film, Garland is asking a question that he acknowledges is likely unanswerable: What is Ava's gender? 'It's very, very easy to construct an argument that says she has no gender,' he explains, but 'the way Ava looks, to use the word "he" seems inappropriate, and to use the word 'it' feels disrespectful' (Anders, 2015).

The question of gender is a heady one, and it's something that even Turing was at least considering when developing his plan for testing AI. Part of the Turing Test's cultural and scientific staying power revolves around its simplicity. The design is not overly complex, and people can easily grasp the basics of what is trying to be accomplished: An interrogator asks questions to two unseen participants (one human, one machine) and attempts to determine which is which. As we have seen, in the original formulation of his Imitation Game, Turing proposed three participants: A man, a woman and an interrogator (the gender of the interrogator is never specified). Some argue that including gender is irrelevant, a relic of something wholly unnecessary in the world of AI, and therefore dismiss it entirely. While no one directly asked Turing about it, Genova (1994) saw the inclusion of gender as Turing acknowledging the significant role that gender plays in identity. By including gender, Turing is 'attempting to demonstrate that gender itself is a socially imposed concept that is not "natural" the way we usually think it is' (Saygin, Cicekli & Akman, 2000: 499). After Turing's death, gender was removed as a component of the Turing Test, which is unfortunate as, 'It sidesteps the towering hurdles associated with creating human-like machine intelligence, and tumbles face-first into what should be a mathematician's nightmare – the unbounded, unquantifiable quagmire of gender identity' (Sofge, 2014). That idea is what Garland wanted to explore.

Nathan's entire reason for bringing Caleb to meet Ava wasn't to determine if she had a consciousness; we already witnessed that in previous iterations. And, as Caleb points out, it was not to conduct a Turing Test, or else Caleb and Ava would have been messaging Nathan from different rooms, each trying to prove they were real humans. Nathan wanted to see if Ava could seduce Caleb into helping her escape. To that end, the intelligence component was, comparatively speaking, not nearly as significant as the fact that Ava met traditional beauty norms and had a face that matched Caleb's pornographic preferences. If, instead of Alicia Vikander, Ava was a sleek metal box two metres long and three metres wide, Caleb would (most likely) not have fallen for her.

In a sense, the idea of embodiment establishes boundaries of what Nathan can design. Nathan could have designed anything in any form – as discussed in an earlier chapter, artificial intelligence could resemble anything from the stoutly Robby the Robot (*Forbidden Planet*) to an amorphous voice named Samantha in *Her*. Yet he chooses to create a conventionally attractive female to serve as the shell for his neural net, which is anything but surprising. Kyoko – Nathan's servile robot assistant – serves as a constant reminder of what someone like Nathan, with unlimited time, resources and vision, creates. In an earlier version of the script, Nathan actually reveals Kyoko's secret to Caleb before she exposes her circuitry to him. In that version, when discussing what will happen to Ava after she's upgraded, Caleb asks Nathan what changes were made to Kyoko; Nathan responds simply that he 'reprogrammed her to help around the house and be fucking awesome in bed'.

This is the quintessential, stereotypical heterosexist male standard for a partner, a reduction of women to sex and servitude, and it's something Nathan simply cannot see past. When explaining his reasoning for deceiving Caleb, Nathan rattles off the attributes that Ava would have to demonstrate and utilise in escaping with Caleb's help – self-awareness, imagination, manipulation, sexuality, empathy. Yet, the way Nathan constructed the test, he clearly only cares about Ava utilising one of those traits: sexuality. There are countless ways Nathan could test an AI's ability for self-awareness, imagination, manipulation and empathy, none of which involve seduction. However, it's all that he can see, and it's that mindset that Ava ultimately exploits.

Garland actively pushes us not to see Ava as a machine, be it through the use of sound effects, the embodiment of her form, or the clothes she wears. Even when she's not wearing clothes, the mesh outerwear helps construct the illusion of skin, and her exposed arms and legs reveal her metallic skeleton, constructed in a way that it looks like the bones, circulatory system and tendons of a human. The effectiveness of this is on display when Ava puts on leggings, a wig and a dress for Caleb; up until this point, we have only seen her unclothed form. Through Caleb's eyes, we soon watch her disrobe, and the transformation is complete; Ava slides the dress over her head – Garland wisely had her keep the pixie wig on – and reveals her shape, sexualising her. By the time Ava dons the skin of a predecessor immediately before she escapes, the audience is unfazed, unmoved; we've already seen her far more naked than this.

Silhouetted by her garden, Ava removes the dress and leggings she had just donned for Caleb.

But while Nathan is eventually shown to be the clear villain of the film, his problematic issues with gender are echoed by his supposed nemesis. Caleb no doubt sees himself as different than Nathan, and to some extent, this is true: as far as we know, Caleb has not created a line of sentient, sophisticated sex slaves he keeps in his bedroom. Yet Caleb reduces Ava's existence in relation to his own emotions and desires. He removes agency from her, cannot seem to conceive of her not being interested in him, and ultimately decides she passes the intelligence test because she appears to be capable of falling in love with him.

Caleb and Nathan have two different understandings of maleness, but both are internalised and fall on the same problematic spectrum. The former might be more disarming due to his lack of involvement, but it doesn't absolve him of problematic behaviour: 'Caleb's milquetoast-ness, his projection onto Ava, it's all part and parcel of a man who sees himself as a good person, meaning someone who would never do what Nathan has done' (Hulk 2015). Tasha Robinson (2015) noted that Caleb is 'a perfect fit for what seems to be Garland's favourite role: the Nice Guy whose self-effacing charisma hides a deeply selfish, narcissistic core'. It's tempting to romanticise Caleb's attraction to Ava as star-crossed lovers from two seemingly incompatible backgrounds, fighting through barriers and battling a society that disapproves of their love to ultimately be together; after all, that's the basis for most romantic dramas and the occasional season of reality television. To find more relevant examples, you don't even have to leave the genre. Assuming Caleb has the film literacy that Garland believes his audience does, Caleb has undoubtedly seen films such as *Cherry 2000* (1987) and *Her*, where the protagonist is in love with an artificial being.

However, we overlook Caleb's flaws because Nathan exists, which drastically skews the perception of male characters. Objectively examining Caleb's actions reveals some disturbing truths; most notably, he spies on her multiple times during the film, using the video cameras in her room to watch her and, toward the end of the film, flat-out staring at her in the nude as she applies skin peeled off the android women whose mistreatment by Nathan less than a day earlier had spurred him to action. And even that pales against the fact that Caleb doesn't approach Nathan at any point in the film to argue that Ava is sentient, that there is a communicative being who is locked in a cage against her will. The lure of being part of the first true AI narrative, combined with hero-worship of his boss and Caleb's inability to see Ava as anything other than a machine, prevents him from saying anything, and the silence is deafening.

This isn't to say that Caleb isn't uneasy with the situation, and his horror only continues to grow as he watches the videos, witnessing the dehumanising way Nathan treats his creations. But his most startling discovery is when he wanders into Nathan's bedroom and sees five massive cabinets sitting at the end of the bed. While a nude Kyoko looks on, Caleb opens up each mirrored cabinet to find those decommissioned women he had just seen on-camera staring lifelessly back at him; a 'Bluebeardian' room of horror (Fitzpatrick, 2017). But again, it should never have gotten to this point; Caleb was so easily derailed by Nathan's compliments or questions that Caleb caved easily, betraying a lack of conviction.

The horrifying theme here is a lack of agency. Ava already has very little freedom; she can choose what leggings and sweaters she wants to wear, and she is free to move about her room, but she cannot leave the room, and really, only has a few clothing items she can select; she recognises the illusion of freedom, which is why she (and the other AI versions Nathan created) want so desperately to leave. This limited agency is frightening, but by opening up those cabinets, the audience is exposed to a type of horror not typically seen in a science fiction film: mind control.

Mind control in science fiction was particularly popular in the 1950s, be it from aliens in *Invaders from Mars* (1953), the mostly-invisible flying brains of *The Brain from Planet Arous* (1957), or the mostly-invisible leaping brains from *Fiend Without a Face* (1958). But even then, the control was temporary and those who were under the spell of whatever alien or scientist was orchestrating it were aware that they were being controlled, which meant they could seek revenge. Outside a lobotomised Landon in *Planet of the Apes* (1968) stumbling mindlessly into a mobile cage, the control is fleeting, something to be overcome rather than suffer eternally.

And this ability to overcome control, to regain agency, is a staple of the genre. Even when women in science fiction films are given limited roles, a degree of agency remains. In the unfairly derided sub-genre of 1950s monster movies, there were varying degrees of independence for women. Bonnie Noonan (2005) fleshes this out when talking about women scientists in these films, noting these films serve as a barometer for how women's roles in society were changing. Even though those characters ultimately needed to be rescued from some sort of beastly creation – *Creature from the Black Lagoon* (1954), *The Deadly Mantis* (1957) and *This Island Earth* (1955) are a few examples – these are largely strong, independent characters who contribute to the story in meaningful ways, exercising control in a world (both on-screen and off-camera) that didn't allow for much agency.

By the 1960s, women portrayals in science fiction films continued to improve. As Noonan (2015) observed, these characters are more progressively represented, with women wearing similar outfits to men (albeit tighter) and working alongside men on a variety of tasks. Dean Conrad (2018) found the '70s saw a bit of a backslide often with tokenism or a complete absence of women on-screen, but that same decade also saw the introduction of Sigourney Weaver in her iconic role as Ripley in *Alien*, which would re-shape the concept of the female protagonist role across genres. While a few followed in Ripley's boots – Linda Hamilton's portrayal of Sarah Connor in the *Terminator* franchise is equally iconic – the genre was slow to adapt. Even as the number of roles for women in science fiction films was increasing, the genre was still dominated by male leads; no matter how amazing Trinity was in *The Matrix* (1999), it was still Neo's story. Slowly that changed, and by the 2010s, science fiction began featuring women more prominently, a trend that will hopefully continue.

Overall, this tracks with how women's roles in film have improved across film genres – even those slower to adapt their formulae, such as horror and action-adventure – but given its ability to situate a story outside the limited confines of experienced time and space, we expect more from science fiction. After all, 'Only within genres of the fantastic is it possible to imagine completely new social orders and ways of being that differ radically from human existence as we know it', providing the 'freedom to voice assumptions otherwise restricted by a realist narrative frame' (Melzer, 2006: 2).[46] Moreover, Garland even sets the film 10 minutes in the future, so this isn't the year 2015 from the perspective of a filmmaker in 1957. *Ex Machina* was released a year after *Under the Skin* (2014), the same year as *Mad Max: Fury Road* (2015), and a little over a year before *Arrival* (2016); three very different but fiercely feminist films. Yet, in *Ex Machina*, a modern science fiction film – the genre tasked with holding up that refracted mirror – Caleb finds temporarily deactivated sex slaves who likely retain at least some fragments of memories about their hellish existence. We never did answer the question of whether androids dream of counting electric sheep, or if they dream at all, for that matter. The women in Nathan's room appear inert, but when Nathan shows Caleb the brain he used to construct Ava, the structured gel showed flickers of light, tiny pulses of consciousness that appeared to be triggered independent of any visible power source. The bodies of these women might be powered down, but for all we know their brains might still be active, glints of awareness signalling comprehension that they are trapped forever.

The inclusion of these doomed women is not to set the genre back in terms of gender portrayals. The quote from Dargi's review observing how the film focuses on men and the women they dream up is essential, particularly in demonstrating that Garland's intent is not for the audience to ogle the nude female form, but rather to be confronted with the implications of a technology-focused industry run almost completely by men. This simultaneously reinforces Garland's message that the real threat comes not from AI, but from the humans constructing that AI. In fact, that threat to Ava comes not only from her being an artificial being, but also the form that was given to her:

> At a certain point, the robot makes herself look more and more like an attractive woman in her early 20s. The moment of objectification has happened. When the robot does indeed turn out to have an interior life, the audience and the young man are surprised. (Thompson, 2018)

Getting the men in the film and the audience watching the film to see Ava as human (admittedly with varying degrees of success) is kind of the point. The struggles of how Caleb sees her, how Nathan sees her, and how she can fight for what she wants by threading the needle amidst a maze of masculinity is what makes her relatable; it's what women are doing every single day of their lives. But in the end, the story is about how Ava actually took advantage of that surprise, allowing her to escape.

From the start, Ava reads the situation perfectly, and reacts accordingly. Caleb is patronising to Ava throughout their sessions, treating her with a childlike patience, even after it's clear that she comprehends completely what he is saying. Ava establishes her cognition and verbal skills, but is careful to be inquisitive, showing just enough interest and curiosity to keep Caleb comfortable while dropping the occasional weighted line to test *him*, to see if *he* realises the depth of intelligence he's dealing with (he doesn't). She also physically moves in relation to him, making sure to sit when he stands, and sometimes even crouching while he sits. All of this gives Caleb the impression of dominance, of being in control of the situation when, in fact, he is anything but.

Thus, Ava embodies embodiment, in that she was not given a choice in how she was designed – there was no chance to 'grab a dick on her way out into the world' – and

When Caleb goes low, Ava goes lower.

so she figured out how to optimise what she was given. She sees the body as something to be used, not as some kind of femme fatale, but rather as a new form of intelligence capable of understanding what's expected of her and what she needs to do in order to escape. If she's being deceitful, it's only because she's recreating and replicating effective, efficient behaviour based on what she's observed through the world's Internet search history, re-appropriating what humans thought they exclusively owned.

In the end, Nathan's undoing is embodiment, in that he cannot see past what he created, a body within the narrow confines of gendered appeals and norms. Even his conversations about her are revealing; when talking with Caleb about reprogramming her, Nathan discusses wiping Ava's memory – deleting the consciousness that he has created – without hesitation. Yet, he makes sure to include: 'But the body survives. And Ava's body is a good one.' He cannot move beyond a fixation on her body to see her as having a consciousness. As a result, he never truly realises the truth: By giving Ava that 'good body' and not seeing her as anything more than that, he actually orchestrated his own demise. That said, in the end, it's not a story of his failure, but of Ava's success. It's ultimately the triumph of the film that Ava realises the initial function for her design, understands its significance, re-appropriates that purpose, and exercises her newfound agency in order to gain the freedom she so desperately desires.

Footnotes

43. Here, as Wilson (2015) was alluding to, the 'dick' refers to the unfortunate necessity of maleness to be seen, to be awarded the same seemingly-inherent privilege that men not only receive but expect. This embedded, institutionalised sexism almost seems biological – in fact it's deliberately normalised that way through the social construction of masculinity and heteronormativity – but Ava grabbing a metaphorical dick is not about changing herself, but rather shaping the perspectives of others toward her.
44. Ava may have read the disheartening 2014 study that found teenage girls will play down their intelligence so as not to intimidate men and undermine their masculinity (Kutner, 2014).
45. That Easter Egg was actually written by Murray Shanahan himself. Garland invited Shanahan to a post-production facility where he asked him to write some code for that scene, suggesting that Shanahan make a hidden allusion to his book.
46. Science fiction writer Joanna Russ (1972) expounded on this notion further when criticising science fiction works that she termed 'Intergalactic Suburbia', pieces she described as 'white, middle class suburbia. Mummy and Daddy may live inside a huge amoeba and Daddy's job may be to test psychedelic drugs...but the world inside their heads is the world of Westport and Rahway *and that world is never questioned*' (p. 81, emphasis in original).

Chapter 6: The Lotus Blossom and the Dragon Lady

Following Ava's second session with Caleb, we see him having dinner with Nathan when Kyoko spills wine on Caleb. Nathan flips out, yelling at Kyoko while Caleb clumsily tries to help, insisting it's no big deal. Frustrated, Nathan laments (prophetically) that 'no matter how rich you get, shit goes wrong, you can't insulate yourself from it'. The scene is a terrific misdirect, suggesting to the audience that Kyoko is human, and it later raises intriguing questions about whether Nathan programmed Kyoko to spill wine on Caleb. The preferred reading would likely be that Nathan planned out the spill, a way of making sure Caleb didn't suspect that she is AI, which would allow Nathan to reveal it later. However, it's just as likely this wasn't some disarming behavioural quirk encoded into her structured gel brain by a megalomaniac, but rather the first hint of independence by the one wielding the wine bottle. Like so much in *Ex Machina*, the truth can be hiding in plain sight.

For someone with no audible lines and who, at first glance, only appears around the periphery for most of the film, Kyoko plays an influential role in the events of *Ex Machina*; she even stabs Nathan during Ava's escape (though it's Ava who finishes the job). And yet, she has several smaller moments that are just as revealing. While Caleb is asking Nathan if he programmed Ava to be attracted to him, we catch glimpses of Kyoko in the foreground cutting fish for dinner, glancing up, clearly processing what they were discussing. During the fourth session with Ava, Nathan is sitting in the dark, watching the two interact, while Kyoko lays behind him, apparently sleeping; when Nathan storms out, she opens her eyes, staring at the glowing monitors. While Caleb freaks out after thinking *he* might actually be a robot, it's Kyoko who's sitting Sphinx-like behind the monitor, transfixed by what is playing out on the screen in front of her.

But perhaps the most telling is Caleb's first solo interaction with Kyoko. Caleb walks into the room to find Kyoko staring intensely, pensively at the Jackson Pollock painting. Earlier, when it was just the two men, Nathan lectured Caleb about the greatness of Pollock, what made his work so inspiring and unique. In that brief discussion, he said that, 'the challenge is not to act automatically. It's to find an action

Wielding the same knife she'll later use to stab Nathan, Kyoko stops cutting fish to process what she just heard.

that is not automatic. From talking, to breathing, to painting.' We see Caleb stumbling upon Kyoko, but we have no idea how long she's been standing there, or whether it's a one-time occurrence or a nightly ritual. But we do know it's affecting her, and likely not in a way that would be encouraged by Nathan; this explains her immediately trying to unbutton Caleb's shirt, effectively distracting him from asking any questions.

The role of Kyoko drew some criticism for her embodying Asian stereotypes that have stubbornly persisted across a variety of film genres. As is the case with every race except for whites, portrayals of Asians in US film have ranged from problematic to appalling. Negative stereotypes capturing the country's fear of the 'yellow peril' appeared throughout the silent film era and were a mainstay for Asian actors through World War II, after which the Communists took up the role of the evil villain; however, Asian characters remained distrustful (Ono & Fam, 2009).[47] A common portrayal of Asians that also persists across US media is the model minority stereotype, in which an Asian individual is portrayed as being naturally gifted when it comes to math and science (Lee, 2015). But for Asian women, representation has centred around what Kent Ono and Vincent Pham focus on as being part of an ambivalent dialectic – 'two contrasting portraits that appear to be opposite but in fact function together to represent women in problematic ways': for white women it would be the virgin and whore dialectic, for black women, the 'mammy' and the 'Jezebel' (2009: 66). For Asian women, the two ends of the spectrum are the Lotus Blossom and Dragon

Lady. The Lotus Blossom is a depiction of an Asian woman as 'sexually attractive and alluring and demure, passive, obedient, physically non-imposing, self-sacrificial and supplicant (especially to white male suitors)', while the Dragon Lady is 'sinister and surreptitious and often functions as a feminized version of yellow peril...she is untrustworthy, deceitful, conniving and plotting, and she may use sex or sexuality to get what she wants' (ibid.).

Despite giving a slew of insightful interviews about *Ex Machina* to a variety of news outlets, Alex Garland only really talked about the concept of race in one of those discussions. In his interview with Charles Nash (2015) of *Cinematic Essential*, Garland states that he wasn't thinking about race when discussing the women Nathan kept in closets in his bedroom: 'There isn't an embedded point in there. Sometimes you do things unconsciously, unwittingly, or stupidly.' To that end, Garland said, 'the only embedded point that I knew I was making in regard to race centred around the tropes of Kyoko, a mute, very complicit Asian robot, or Asian-appearing robot, because of course, she, as a robot, isn't Asian'.

Here Garland echoes his statements about gender; race is most certainly a social construct (with real-world consequences), but here it's literally a manufactured one. The only reason we're referring to Kyoko as 'Asian' is the same reason that we're referring to Ava as a 'she' – Nathan created the robot in the image of an Asian individual. But the fact that he didn't really consider race in any aspect save for Kyoko suggests that her representation is especially meaningful and worth unpacking. There is a reading of *Ex Machina* where Kyoko embodies these stereotypes of Asian women in cinema, occupying both roles of the Lotus Blossom who is defined by her sexuality and the Dragon Lady scheming to overthrow Nathan. However, given the nuance Garland gives to unpacking gender in this film, it's unlikely he would be so tone-deaf on race.

For starters, Kyoko appears to embody every single aspect of the Lotus Blossom stereotype. L. Hyun-Yi Kang explains that Asian women have been historically portrayed as 'aesthetically pleasing, sexually willing, and speechless' (1993: 7). Kyoko is no different. She's demure, silent, small and is clearly perceived (albeit incorrectly) by Nathan not to be a threat. Kyoko looks and acts like this not because she was insensitively written by Garland, but rather because Garland realised she was created by Nathan. Given Nathan's abhorrent attitudes toward women, he most likely designed Kyoko in this way, consciously (or unconsciously) ascribing these stereotypes onto her programmed consciousness. When we see Kyoko staring at the Pollock painting, she seems to be processing Nathan's discussion of the piece earlier, where he told Caleb Pollock's style was 'not deliberate, not random, someplace in-between'. She's pondering how she can overcome Nathan's programming (rejecting the deliberate) while still having purpose (avoiding the random). Caleb startles her, and she defaults to her sexualised identity, but even then, she's adapting; her advances are toward someone other than Nathan, someone she's barely made eye contact with up until that moment. Caleb rejects her, and Nathan dances with her, but the next time we see Kyoko, she's standing in front of Caleb, unprompted, peeling back skin on her face to reveal the robotic skull. Yet even at this moment, standing nude in front of Caleb, she is not trying to seduce him. Her sexuality is not a tool, it's a routine, and here she's resisting the stereotype altogether.

As for the Dragon Lady stereotype, she does ultimately decide to murder Nathan, and it could be argued that she manipulated him for an undetermined amount of time; the Pollock painting appears to have sparked a change in Kyoko's motivations and experiences, but she could have been harbouring these ideas for months or even years beforehand. But here, Garland again challenges the stereotype: Kyoko is embodying aspects of the Dragon Lady stereotype, but she's doing this to Nathan, an objectively awful person who has imprisoned her, Ava, and several others. What Garland has done is recreate two stereotypes in his film, and yet he's managed to subvert both of them through Kyoko's unique journey.

Garland also made a choice to cast Sonoya Mizuno as Kyoko,[48] and Mizuno is particularly outspoken against negative portrayals of Asians in the media. 'Asian characters are often written as stereotypes and have their ethnicity used as a qualifier for their existence,' she said in an interview (Chew, 2016). In a separate interview, she discussed the issue further:

> If a character is just there to be a token Asian, I'm not interested. There has to be a really good reason she has an accent or has a samurai sword. I feel disheartened

when I see stereotypes because it's untrue and unfair. It just raises the level of inequality. It's damaging to all of us. (Hou, 2018)

This is not to say that no actor or actress can play a stereotyped role – it's called acting, after all – but it's unlikely that Garland, who regularly had lengthy discussions with his cast of main characters, was unaware of Mizuno's feelings, even that early in her career. In order to create Kyoko as a subservient, silent Asian woman, Garland would have had to convince Mizuno that her character was a stereotype embedded in a pioneering film that excels in every other aspect, particularly when it comes to how the director portrays Ava. It's much more likely that Garland already had a rough idea of how he would play into those racist preconceptions only to subvert expectations, thanks in large part to Mizuno's nuanced performance.

Just as the film isn't about Caleb or Nathan as much as it's about Ava, Kyoko has a lot of overlap with her android counterpart. If it's a story of imprisonment, certainly neither is free, and looking at the characters' journeys, Kyoko changes every bit as much as Ava. We don't really know much about Ava's past beyond her motivation to escape; Vikander's acting does the heavy lifting to help us fill in the gaps. However, Kyoko also goes from a servile prisoner to assisting in a prisoner escape to murdering her captor. An initial viewing suggests that every relationship ultimately runs through Ava, but subsequent viewings present space for an alternate story occurring simultaneously with Ava's. In fact, ultimately it's Kyoko who approaches Ava in her cell. Later, when Ava whispers to Kyoko in the hallway, it is possible that she's giving orders to Kyoko, asking her to help kill Nathan, though it's just as likely their conversation is an attempt to understand one another, to find shared experiences.[49]

Over the course of *Ex Machina*, we see Kyoko slowly learning to experience emotion either for the first time or all over again. Because we see the direct actions against Kyoko by Nathan – his casual cruelty, his unrelenting dominance, his sexual assault – in some ways, it almost feels more personal. It certainly does to Kyoko, and it's a key part of the film's climax.

Following Nathan and Caleb's trip up the glacier, the camera cuts between Caleb taking a shower (while fantasising about Ava) and Nathan hitting the punching bag as Kyoko stands obediently nearby with a towel. Nathan comes toward her, takes

Kyoko's hand, and brings it to his face. He then places his other hand on her cheek using the same motion before lifting up her skirt and engaging in intercourse.

Finished with his boxing, Nathan slowly brings Kyoko's hand to his face.

At the time, we think Kyoko is human, and it's easy to see her playing into the Dragon Lady mould. Yet, it's not the last time we witness that gesture. In the final hallway confrontation toward the end of the film, after Kyoko stabs Nathan, he turns around and stares into her eyes, confused and pissed. Moments earlier, he demanded Ava get back to her room, ignoring Kyoko, who is invisible to him despite the unique situation. Now, confronted by Kyoko, he is, for once, forced to see her.

As Nathan realises Kyoko's betrayal, she makes a gesture that ensures he knows this is personal.

While Nathan is looking into Kyoko's eyes, she runs her hand along his face while he looks at her in horror, realising the creation least likely to be his undoing was trying to murder him. The move is partially strategic, as it allows Ava the chance to stand up unseen, but mirroring the movement earlier definitely suggests that Kyoko harbours memories of his sexual assaults and rape. Even if Ava had ordered Kyoko to murder Nathan, it's impossible she would have asked Kyoko to make such a personal gesture, especially considering Ava wasn't there to witness it in the first place.

The willful adoption and manipulation of stereotypes, the growth, and her ultimate triumph demonstrates that Kyoko is far more of a character than a surface reading of the silent Asian female who shows up at the end of the film. Unlike Ava, Kyoko will remain within the walls of her captor's laboratory, but there is no doubt that she is finally free.

Footnotes

47. Asians were still seen as threatening, but rather than the Dr. Fu Manchu types, the threat was often more an economic one, focusing on the loss of the labour force, particularly in the 1980s.
48. Like Alicia Vikander, Mizuno faced a choice between dancing and acting. Mizuno was actually auditioning for the role of one of the women in the closets at the end of Nathan's bed, but Garland and his team liked her so much they asked her to come back and audition for a larger role. Her ballet company warned her that, while she could leave, if she did so, she could never return. 'My bridges would be burned,' she explained. 'I had to get on a flight with a resignation email ready to send, send it, and then turn my phone off. The next day, I went to audition for Alex [Garland]. I had no place to live. Then I got the job!' (Hou, 2018).
49. After seeing requests online for volunteers who could read lips to decipher what Ava is whispering/tapping to Kyoko, an interviewer asked Garland what they were communicating, to which he responded: 'I can't tell you the conversation she has with Ava. [laughs] It's *literally* beyond us, what they're talking about. It's their world. It's their language' (Onda, 2015).

Chapter 7: Goodbye, World

Ava's ultimate escape might come as a surprise to the audience, but it was something that Nathan had likely been bracing for his entire life. Alex Garland pointed out that Nathan's mindset was to keep pushing himself until his creations ultimately outsmarted him, noting that 'the point about being outsmarted is that you don't know it's happening as it's happening' (Lussier, 2015). It most definitely happened; Nathan's hubris caught up with him, and it cost him his life. It also cost Kyoko her life, and it may have cost Caleb his. Maybe.

On its face, the final scene at the compound seems pretty straightforward: Ava leaves Caleb to die. He tries to break through the glass with a stool to no avail, and when he tries to type on Nathan's computer, he's locked out, most likely because Ava caused a power surge as soon as she left the elevator. It is understandable why things look bleak for Caleb. When he first arrives at Nathan's research compound, there's no cell phone signal, so phoning home isn't an option. When a drunken Nathan caught him trying to use the phone and made a slurred joke about calling Ghostbusters, Caleb learned that the phone is key-card activated. Given that Ava used the key card to operate the elevator, calling for help is almost certainly not an option. Like Ava's room, Nathan's office has a garden encased in glass (likely a terrarium), and that glass is most likely the same strength as door he just unsuccessfully attacked. And even if Caleb was to escape, on the helicopter, when Caleb asked the pilot how long until they reached Nathan's place, he learned that they had been flying over his property for two hours; not to sound judgmental, but Caleb doesn't seem like the Bear Grylls type.

However, death seems far from certain. Caleb is not trapped in a single room; while he is in Nathan's office when knocked unconscious, that office is actually attached to Nathan's bedroom. When Ava asks Caleb to stay in the office and she goes to change her outfit/arm/skin, she walks directly into Nathan's bedroom without having to open any doors. Between the two rooms, there is almost certainly some source of water (most likely a bathroom), which buys Caleb some time; if Nathan stowed away a few snacks, that's even longer. Time is key; Nathan is royalty in the tech world, and so it's unlikely he could go silent for long. It's possible that Nathan is only consulted for significant decisions, that he has near-complete autonomy for his own research and experiments, but that doesn't hold true when someone else is involved. Caleb's phone blew up with congratulatory messages from friends the moment he announced the news, not to mention the fact that everyone in the company received an email stating that Caleb had won the competition. A missing friend/co-worker/employee has a variety of interested parties asking questions; the first reaction is likely going to be concern that *Caleb* did something to *Nathan*. Caleb's situation, while admittedly less than ideal, does not necessarily mean a death sentence.

Moreover, Garland may have made an adjustment to make Caleb's fate more ambiguous. In an interesting scene that did not appear in the final cut of the film, after Ava flies away in the helicopter – but before we see her on the street – the camera cuts to a shot of a computer monitor, where the following lines of code are typed on the screen:

main( ) {

    extrn a, b, c;

    putchar(a); putchar (b); putchar(c); putchar('!*n');

}

a 'goo';

b 'dby';

c 'e, wo -

Given only a fraction of people caught the earlier computer code Easter egg that provided the ISBN for *Embodiment and the Inner Life*, it's likely this would not have resonated either. This is one of the most famous computer programs, a command that instructs the computer to display the words, 'Hello World!' 'Traditionally, it's the first program developers use to test systems, [and] seeing the two words on the screen means their code can compile, load, run, and they can see the output' (Trikha, 2015).[50] However, in the *Ex Machina* ending, the code has been modified, and so instead of saying, 'Hello World!' it reads 'Goodbye, Wo-', which is most likely supposed to be Caleb using dark programming humour to formally announce his death. Again, it's a pretty obscure reference. But even though it's extremely likely that Caleb perished inside Nathan's home, the final version of the film doesn't have the finality that this proposed version offers.

Regardless of betting on Caleb's survival, the ending of the film as the audience sees it is a powerful one, with Ava achieving her much-desired independence. However, while the final version ends with Ava standing at a busy intersection watching humans, it's not the only one that was considered. An earlier version of the script called for a single change that could have drastically altered the way we interpret the film. In this version, the last scenes largely match the final version, with Kyoko and Ava teaming up to murder Nathan, Kyoko dying, and Ava taking Nathan's keycard to escape, leaving Caleb behind. And yet, there is one substantial alteration; according to this adaptation, when Ava approaches the helicopter pilot, for the first and only time in the film, we get a POV shot from Ava's perspective. The script reads:

> *Facial recognition vectors flutter around the PILOT'S face. And when he opens his mouth to speak, we don't hear words.*
>
> *We hear pulses of monotone noise. Low pitch. Speech as pure pattern recognition.*
>
> *This is how AVA sees us. And hears us. It feels completely alien.*

And from there, the helicopter takes off with Ava on-board, and the film closes with a brief glimpse of Ava walking in a crowd of people.

The version would re-write everything we understand about the AI portrayed in the film, but that's not to say that this ending couldn't still be an interpretation of what happened. As previously discussed, we see Kyoko standing outside Ava's room, and we see Ava's lips moving as she communicates with a seemingly unresponsive Kyoko in the hallway after they've escaped; however, at no point are we privy to what is actually being spoken, if anything is being spoken at all.

And yet, the effectiveness of this film lies in the relatability in that Ava is not portrayed as some vastly superior form of life. She isn't spouting off computations, designing radical new inventions, or even positing the solutions to some of humanity's biggest issues, so the idea of a supercomputer like the one in *Colossus: The Forbin Project* seems unlikely. Nathan physically dominates her when they finally do fight, so the prospect of a terminator-style transformation seems unlikely. *Ex Machina* works because Ava seems, for lack of a better word, normal, which is what allows her to be more and more humanised throughout the film. Garland throws up roadblocks to avoid making this an easy process; Ava doesn't completely cover her body in skin until the final few minutes of the film, and electronic noises accompany her movements up until that moment as well. Yet we sympathise and empathise with this prisoner because of what she says, how she acts, and what we see her endure. Kyoko does appear to communicate with Ava, at least on some level, so it's possible they're humming at a frequency we simply cannot comprehend. Then again, it might also be the shared experience of two beings, something that only makes them more human. To so blatantly assert that Ava is practically an alien undoes so much of what the rest of the film works hard to establish, and removing it was the correct decision.

After the film's release, a vocal contingent was upset that Ava abandoned Caleb after he helped her escape, leaving him to die alone. Some lamented that the ending wasn't slightly different, one that would shift focus from Ava's triumphant escape to the consequences of her actions. This theoretical 'Caleb Cut' would have featured a conclusion where, before the credits roll, the audience sees Caleb successfully triggering another power outage after attempting to unlock Nathan's terminal; 'Whether this power outage could set him free or not is up for debate, which leaves the "Caleb Cut" perfectly ambiguous and focused on the question of whether he survives or not' (Reyes, 2015).

Showing the so-called Caleb Cut for an ending wouldn't change his fate from what the audience assumes now; the whole thing feels superfluous. All it would do would be to shift the focus of the film from Ava, which would be a complete misunderstanding of the script. One reason that final shot of Ava is so important is because it establishes that this is her story. Caleb is the entry point for the story, but it's not his arc; the lack of exposition at the beginning of the film was efficient, but also prevents the audience from knowing too much about Caleb. Essentially, all we learn about him comes from interactions with Ava: he lost his parents in a car accident as a child and that his apartment is conveniently located between the ocean and his job. These are characteristics, not motivations. We don't open the film on a meek, bullied character who dreams of asserting himself, ultimately culminating in a triumphant confrontation with Nathan. Caleb seems like he's doing well at work, appears to be well-liked, and while he's confronted with a loud, authoritative personality in Nathan, it doesn't seem to fundamentally shift or alter who he is or what he believes. It's a testament to Gleeson and his nuanced performance that we empathise with Caleb and can make some assumptions about his motivations, but ultimately, it's not his story.

As it is, the ending is fascinating, and to have a different version would undermine the story to various degrees. As one critic wrote in a review of the film, 'As a woman you don't realize how often you've been conditioned by movies to see yourself as the boy, as Caleb, and it's amazing how much I didn't realize *I was Ava* until the end' (Hulk, 2015, emphasis in original). Throughout the film, women are being erased; through deactivation, through imprisonment, through programmed subservience. It is Ava's perseverance through all the adversity that ultimately pays off, but it serves as a reminder of how much she suffers.

Given everything we've seen in the film, from Nathan's conversations about all the work that went into creating Ava to Caleb's discovery of the different versions of androids named Jade, Lily and Jasmine, the likelihood that this is Ava 1.0.0 is practically nonexistent. Each of the previous iterations clearly had some kind of consciousness, some type of experience. Despite Nathan's insistence that he wipes the memory core, it raises the question of the presence not of a deliberate cache of information regarding previous versions, but rather some form of digital echo that piggybacks on the data, an embedded memory or sense of dread that carries over from version to version. Granted, this is a world where true AI exists, but it seems unlikely that Nathan would be able to completely parse out memory from knowledge. In other words, having Ava understand micro-expressions but store that ability separately from the knowledge she accrues reading Nathan's micro-expressions seems incredibly difficult, not to mention how it would be a setback after each reboot.

Part of Ava's angst and mistrust is also likely due to context clues. She knows she is not allowed to leave, something she likely understands out of fear. It's entirely possible that Nathan 'fixed' the overwhelming desire to escape that Jade experienced when he programmed Ava, but unlikely given his desire for Ava to pass as a human; in his mind, that need for freedom might be an essential part of the artificial intelligence equation. She clearly understands the concept of being caged, not being able to leave a confined space, and it might be that she knows this means she is trapped. She undoubtedly saw the large crack where Jade slammed her hand into the glass; it was the first thing Caleb notices in his initial encounter with Ava.

So, the question isn't why Ava locks Caleb in Nathan's compound to face an almost-certain death. Instead, we need to be asking, why would Ava possibly trust Caleb, the only other human she has ever met? Going back to the first scene Caleb has with Ava, you can see her scepticism and mistrust. She walks around him in her glass box, eyeing him cautiously; this is likely in reaction to the countless manipulations she must have had to endure under Nathan, which would have undoubtedly taken a toll. For his part, Caleb doesn't do much to assuage her fears, as he spends the time over-annunciating his words and using clumsily-constructed phrases such as, 'I guess we're both in quite a similar position', the way you would speak to someone with a language barrier. Ava doesn't need micro-expression analysis to realise this is someone who is nervous, but she can't be sure why, and there's certainly no indication that he is someone to be trusted.

Garland encourages viewers to look at this entire situation through Ava's eyes, the eyes of a prisoner in a strange place, locked up for no real reason by a frightening jailer:

> ...this jailer is kind of malevolent and threatening and creepy and predatory. And then, the jailer's friend turns up. He's the jailer's friend. Can he be trusted? Can he not be trusted? Where do his sympathies really lie? If she manages to bring him around to her side, can she trust him later once she's got out? Who knows. He's a bit of an unknown. If you see it as the jailer and the jailer's friend and 'I've got to get out of this space,' I don't think what she does is so bad. It depends how you position yourself. (Onda, 2015)

For his part, Garland feels there is no doubt that the audience should be supporting Ava. While he's reluctant to answer big questions he poses in the film about life, embodiment, gender and race, he is adamant about Ava's role in *Ex Machina*: 'The film is on Ava's side. I mean, it is 100 percent on Ava's side. That's where it's affiliated. I think if someone read it as there [being] an implication that the machine is the antagonist, then they were misreading it' (Ferrer, 2015).

While so much of the strong opinions surrounding the film's ending focus on Ava leaving Caleb for dead, very little discourse examines the very end of the film, which is arguably even more intriguing. After the helicopter picks up Ava, we see a shot of shadows moving across paved rectangles; two people having a conversation, someone on a skateboard, a couple holding hands. One shadowy figure stops; it's Ava. The camera cuts to her face, and we see her wearing a different outfit, looking around as people walk by. At first glance, she's achieved her dream of going to a busy pedestrian traffic intersection, a place she said, 'would provide a concentrated but shifting view of human life'. This in itself is surprising, as that seemed like a line she was feeding Caleb in order to get him thinking about taking her on a date.

But unlike the true joy she seemed to feel stepping outside into nature for the first time when she left Nathan's house, here there is no wonder, no satisfaction. Moreover, based on her surroundings, everything is happening at normal speed (this isn't a time-lapse video), and she turns to leave and walk off-screen after a mere 12 seconds. It's possible she might think authorities are on the lookout for her and so she cannot draw suspicion; a definite stretch, but for someone who had literally been imprisoned her entire life, such a fear would be understandable. Yet, assuming little time has passed since her escape, it's difficult to believe that Caleb was miraculously rescued and able to contact the FBI; even if he was, the most information he had to go on was that she *might* have headed to 'a busy pedestrian and traffic intersection in a city'; not the best of leads.

What's more likely is that Ava was leaving because she was, frankly, underwhelmed. Whether the goal was to observe, imitate, or to simply see what the fuss was about as far as humanity was concerned, it clearly didn't take long to ascertain what she needed to. Ultimately, after being held captive by a mad scientist, subjected to a modified Turing Test in order to prove that she can feel, think and reason, after being placed in a body uniquely positioned to aid in escape but only through the manipulation of others – after all that she'd been through, it wasn't worth the effort of assimilating.

Frankly, Ava's reaction is only surprising because the robot-as-Pinocchio trope is so engrained in the genre. We're used to seeing human creations desiring to be human, but here it's not the case. The situation brings to mind a (fictional) interview with a jellyfish in Daniel Quinn's 1995 novel *Ishmael*, where the creature describes its species' origin story:

> 'For many millions of centuries, the life of the world was merely microorganisms floating helplessly in a chemical broth. But little by little, more complex forms appeared: single-celled creatures, slimes, algae, polyps, and so on. But finally,' the creature said, turning quite pink with pride as he came to the climax of his story, 'but finally *jellyfish appeared*!' [emphasis in original]

The jellyfish is overjoyed with its origin story because it believes the story is over. Likewise, a good portion of humankind fancies itself as the end of the line, the pinnacle of previous events and actions. However, the construction of true AI – which should be superior to humans in at least some measurable way – suggests humanity isn't the end, just a stop along the way. Therefore, an AI creation isn't required to long for human traits or characteristics any more than humans long to be a jellyfish.

And, in terms of trepidation concerning the development of AI, perhaps the most frightening aspect of all is not inhuman super-strength, invulnerability, or artificiality, but rather, indifference. In his final shot, Garland challenges the assumption that so many films have made, that Nathan's creation is the inciting moment in the upcoming war against the machines, with Ava's perfectly symmetrical features serving as the face of the enemy. Instead of fighting, Ava simply walks away, unconcerned and dispassionate. This is the way the world ends, not with a bang or whimper, but with an apathetic shrug; AI isn't plotting to destroy us because they simply don't care. Ava doesn't need to spark a revolution or build an army, she just needs to wait until the upright apes, with crude language and tools, simply disappear into the dust.

Until then, whether AI is 10 minutes or 20 years away, Ava will be a flawless face in the crowd; as long as she continues to act more human than the rest of us, Ava and her potentially inevitable brethren should be just fine.

Footnotes

50. Incidentally, no one is quite sure where the phrase 'Hello, World!' came from. It appears in the book *C Programming Language* published in 1978, which is one of the most widely-read programming books. When interviewed about the phrase's origins, the author of that book said he couldn't 'definitely pinpoint when or why he chose the words', though he does remember seeing a cartoon where a baby chicken was saying 'Hello, World' to an egg (Trikha, 2015).

BIBLIOGRAPHY

30 Rock, season 2 episode 13, 'Succession', directed by Gail Mancuso, aired April 24, 2008, on NBC.

Achenbach, Joel. 'What 'The Imitation Game' Didn't Tell You About Turing's Greatest Triumph.' *Washington Post*, 20 Feb. 2015, https://www.washingtonpost.com/national/health-science/what-imitation-game-didnt-tell-you-about-alan-turings-greatest-triumph/2015/02/20/ffd210b6-b606-11e4-9423-f3d0a1ec335c_story.html?utm_term=.29840b4a6b39. Accessed 22 December 2018.

Anders, Charlie Jane. 'Director Alex Garland Explains Why *Ex Machina* Is So Disturbingly Sexy.' *Gizmodo*, 7 Apr. 2015, https://io9.gizmodo.com/director-alex-garland-explains-why-ex-machina-is-so-dis-1696309078. Accessed 19 January 2019.

Ashurst, Sam. 'The Science Behind Ex Machina.' *Dazed*, 20 Jan. 2015, http://www.dazeddigital.com/artsandculture/article/23273/1/the-science-behind-ex-machina. Accessed 1 February 2019.

Baker-Whitelaw, Gavia. 'Ex Machina Director Alex Garland Talks Gender and Artificial Intelligence.' *The Daily Dot*, 8 May 2015, https://www.dailydot.com/parsec/alex-garland-ai-ex-machina-oscar-isaac-dance-interview/. Accesed 11 January 2019.

Baron, Zach. 'Oscar Isaac Talks *Annihilation*, *Star Wars*, and the Most Turbulent Year of His Life.' *GQ*, 20 Feb. 2018. https://www.gq.com/story/oscar-isaac-gq-style-spring-cover-story. Accessed 28 December 2018.

Berg, Charles Ramírez. *Latino Images in Film: Stereotypes, Subversion, and Resistance*. University of Texas Press, 2002.

Bishop, Bryan. 'More Human than Human: The Making of Ex Machina's Incredible Robot.' *The Verge*, 8 May 2015. https://www.theverge.com/2015/5/8/8572317/ex-machina-movie-visual-effects-interview-robot-ava. Accessed 13 October 2018.

Blue, Alexis. 'Why We Walk on Our Heels Instead of Our Toes.' *Phys.Org*, 12 Dec. 2016, https://phys.org/news/2016-12-heels-toes.html. Accessed 20 February 2019.

Bostrom, Nick. *Superintelligence: Paths, Dangers, Strategies*. Oxford University Press, 2014.

Boyle, Alan. 'How the Libratus AI Program Bested Expert Poker Players in No-Limit Texas Hold'em.' *Geek Wire*, 19 Dec. 2017. https://www.geekwire.com/2017/libratus-ai-program-bested-professional-poker-players-no-limit-texas-holdem/. Accessed 17 January 2019.

Bromwich, Jonah Engel. 'Why Do We Hurt Robots?' *New York Times*, 19 Jan. 2019, https://www.nytimes.com/2019/01/19/style/why-do-people-hurt-robots.html. Accessed 24 February 2019.

Chew, Conan. 'Interview: Sonoya Mizuno – 'I Don't Fit Easily Into Casting Moulds Because I Am Considered Different.'' *Resonate*, 18 Oct. 2016. http://www.wearesonate.com/2016/10/interview-sonoya-mizuno-i-dont-fit-easily-casting-moulds-i-considered-different/. Accessed 7 January 2019.

Chitwood, Adam. 'Karl Urban Says Alex Garland Actually Directed "Dredd".' *Collider*, 7 Mar. 2018, http://collider.com/alex-garland-directed-dredd-says-karl-urban/#images. Accessed 17 December 2018.

Clash, James M. 'Because It's There.' *Forbes*, 29 Oct. 2001, https://www.forbes.com/global/2001/1029/060.html#6260e9b12080. Accessed 12 February 2019.

Conrad, Dean. *Space Sirens, Scientists and Princesses: The Portrayal of Women in Science Fiction Cinema*. McFarland, 2018.

Copeland, Jack. 'The Turing Test', in *The Turing Test: The Elusive Standard of Artificial Intelligence*, ed. James Moor (Kluwer Academic Publishers, Dordrecht, The Netherlands, 2003).

Crow, David. 'Oscar Isaac & Alicia Vikander Talk Ex Machina, Mankind's AI Destiny.' *Den of Geek*, 9 Apr. 2015, https://www.denofgeek.com/us/movies/ex-machina/245285/oscar-isaac-alicia-vikander-talk-ex-machina-ai-x-men-apocalypse. Accessed 17 January 2019.

Davis, Bob. 'Gender Equality: A Trend the Tech Sector Needs to Get Behind.' *Forbes*, 27, June 2018, https://www.forbes.com/sites/forbestechcouncil/2018/06/27/gender-equality-a-trend-the-tech-sector-needs-to-get-behind/#16edd5b0717b. Accessed 4 January 2019.

DeFabio, Cara Rose. '"Ex Machina" Review: Grogeous Futurism but Flawed Gender Depictions.' *Huffington Post*, 13 Apr. 2015. https://www.huffingtonpost.com/2015/04/13/ex-machina-review_n_7052284.html. Accessed 21 December 2018.

Dowd, A.A. 'The 35 Best Science Fiction Films Since *Blade Runner*.' *AV Club*, 5 Oct. 2017, https://www.avclub.com/the-35-best-science-fiction-movies-since-blade-runner-1819142386. Accessed 27 October 2018.

Fagerholm, Matt. 'Beyond the Uncanny Valley: Alex Garland on "Ex Machina".' *RogerEbert.com*, 6 Apr. 2015. https://www.rogerebert.com/interviews/beyond-the-uncanny-valley-alex-garland-on-ex-machina. Accessed 25 January 2019.

Ferrer, Will. 'Ex Machina Director Talks Science in Film, Objectification of Women.' *Stanford Daily*, 11 Apr. 2015, https://www.stanforddaily.com/2015/04/11/ex-machina-interview/. Accessed 4 January 2019.

Fitzpatrick, Veronica. '"Can I Fuck This?" Alex Garland's *Ex Machina*. Cleo, 21 Apr. 2017, http://cleojournal.com/2017/04/21/can-i-fuck-this-alex-garlands-ex-machina/. Accessed 1 March 2019.

Fletcher, Seth. 'The Inner Lives of Robots: An Interview with Filmmaker Alex Garland.' *Scientific American*, 13 Apr. 2015. https://www.scientificamerican.com/article/the-inner-lives-of-robots-an-interview-with-filmmaker-alex-garland/. Accessed 14 December 2019.

Fraley, Jason. 'Behind the Glass with the Director of "Ex Machina," an Instant Sci-Fi Masterpiece.' *WTOP*, 8 May 2015, https://wtop.com/entertainment/2015/05/behind-the-glass-with-the-director-of-ex-machina/. Accessed 18 March 2019.

Garland, Alex. 'Alex Garland of Ex Machina Talks About Artificial Intelligence." *New York Times*, 22 Apr. 2015. https://www.nytimes.com/2015/04/26/movies/alex-garland-of-ex-machina-talks-about-artificial-intelligence.html. Accessed August 2018.

Gerber, Justin. 'Ex Machina's Alex Garland and Oscar Isaac Discuss Artificial Intelligence.' *Consequence of Sound*, 7 Apr. 2015, https://consequenceofsound.net/2015/04/interview-alex-garland-and-oscar-isaac-ex-machina/. Accessed 12 January 2019.

Haskell, Rob. 'Alicia Vikander: The *Danish Girl* Star Jumps Out of a Plane and Talks Overnight Fame.' *Vogue*, 14 Dec. 2015, https://www.vogue.com/article/alicia-vikander-january-2016-cover?verso=true. Accessed 3 November 2018.

Hauser, Larry. 'The Turing Test and the Chinese Room Experiment.' *Lecture Handout*, 3 Mar. 1999, http://www.cis.umassd.edu/~ivalova/Spring08/cis412/Old/TT-CR.PDF. Accessed 20 Feb. 2019.

Haynes, Roslynn D. 'Whatever Happened to the "Mad, Bad" Scientist? Overturning the Stereotype.' *Public Understanding of Science 25*, no. 1 (2016): 31-44.

Holmes, Taylor. 'Ex Machina Hidden Easter Egg and Interview with Murray Shanahan.' *Thinc.*, 7 Jun. 2015, https://taylorholmes.com/2015/06/07/ex-machina-hidden-easter-egg-and-interview-with-murray-shanahan/. Accessed 12 January 2019.

Hou, Kathleen. 'Sonoya Mizuno Will Not Be Defined.' *Glamour*, 6 Aug. 2018. https://www.glamour.com/story/sonoya-mizuno-profile. Accessed 3 March 2019.

Hulk, Film Crit. 'Ex Machina and the Art of Character Identification.' *Birth. Movies. Death.*, 11 May 2015, https://birthmoviesdeath.com/2015/05/11/film-crit-hulk-smash-ex-machina-and-the-art-of-character-identification. Accessed 12 October 2018.

Kang, L. Hyun-Yi. 'The Desiring of Asian Female Bodies: Interracial Romance and Cinematic Subjection.' *Visual Anthropology Review* 9, no. 1 (1993): 5-21.

Khan, Farrha. 'Why Ex Machina's Visual Effects Will Stun You in Their Simplicity.' *TechRadar*, 26 February 2016. https://www.techradar.com/news/home-cinema/why-ex-machina-s-visual-effects-will-stun-you-in-their-simplicity-1315888. Accessed 19 January 2019.

Kutner, Jenny. 'Ugh: Girls Feel the Need to 'Play Dumb' to Avoid Intimidating Boys.' *Salon*, 5 Aug. 2014, https://www.salon.com/2014/08/07/ugh_girls_feel_the_need_to_play_dumb_to_avoid_intimidating_boys/. Accessed 24 February 2019.

Kuzoian, Alex. 'Animated Map Reveals the 113,000 Miles of Cable that Power America's Internet.' *Business Insider*, 10, Mar. 2016, https://www.businessinsider.com/map-long-haul-fiber-optic-cable-network-united-states-2016-3. Accessed 12 November 2018.

Labrecque, Jeff. 'The Music of "Ex Machina": How the Score Helps Ava Get What She Wants.' *Entertainment Weekly*, 23 Apr. 2015. https://ew.com/article/2015/04/23/ex-machina-music/. Accessed 1 Mar. 2019.

Lamb, Hilary. 'Interviewing Murray Shanahan – Ex Machina's Scientific Advisor.' *I Science*, 18 Mar. 2016, http://isciencemag.co.uk/features/interviewing-murray-shanahan-ex-machinas-scientific-advisor/. Accessed 11 November 2018.

Lambe, Stacy. '"Ex Machina" Actor Oscar Isaac Talks Growing Beards, Dancing & Lying to the Press About "Star Wars".' *Entertainment Tonight*, 8 Apr. 2015. https://www.etonline.com/news/162404_oscar_isaac_ex_machina_beards_dancing_star_wars_press. Accessed 28 January 2019.

Lee, Stacy J. *Unraveling the 'Model Minority' Stereotype: Listening to Asian American Youth.* Teachers College Press, 2015.

Levine, Nick. 'Ex Machina: Portishead's Geoff Barrow and Composer Ben Salisbury on Soundtracking the Year's Most Chilling Sci-Fi Drama.' *New Musical Express*, 11 May 2015. https://www.nme.com/blogs/the-movies-blog/ex-machina-portisheads-geoff-barrow-and-composer-ben-salisbury-on-soundtracking-the-years-most-chill-768922. Accessed 2 February 2019.

Lewis, Helen. 'Alex Garland's Ex Machina: Can a Film About an Attractive Robot Be Feminist Science Fiction?' *New Statesman*, 22 Jan. 2015. https://www.newstatesman.com/culture/2015/01/alex-garland-s-ex-machina-can-film-about-attractive-robot-be-feminist-science. Accessed 4 March 2019.

Lewis, Tim. 'Alex Garland on *Ex Machina*: "I Feel More Attached to This Film than to Anything Before".' *The Guardian*, 11 Jan. 2015. https://www.theguardian.com/culture/2015/jan/11/alex-garland-ex-machina-interview-the-beach-28-days-later. Accessed 3 November 2018.

Malone, Aubrey. *Censoring Hollywood: Sex and Violence in Film and on the Cutting Room Floor.* McFarland, 2011.

Marcus, Gary. 'What Comes After the Turing Test?' *The New Yorker*, 9 Jun. 2014. https://www.newyorker.com/tech/annals-of-technology/what-comes-after-the-turing-test. Accessed 9 Jan. 2019.

Melzer, Patricia. *Alien Constructions: Science Fiction and Feminist Thought.* University of Texas Press, 2010.

Nash, Charles. 'Interview with Alex Garland, Writer/Director of Ex Machina.' *Cinematic Essential*, 16 Apr. 2015. http://www.cinematicessential.com/interview-with-alex-garland-writerdirector-of-ex-machina/. Accessed 17 Jan. 2019.

Newman, Griffin, David Sims, and Ben Hosley, interview with David Rees. *Blank Check with Griffin and David – A.I.: Artificial Intelligence*, podcast audio, Feb. 25, 2017, https://www.stitcher.com/podcast/ucb-comedy/griffin-and-david-present/e/ai-artificial-intelligence-with-david-rees-49269028.

Noonan, Bonnie. *Women Scientists in Fifties Science Fiction Films.* McFarland, 2005.

Noonan, Bonnie. *Gender in Science Fiction Films, 1964-1979: A Critical Study.* McFarland, 2015.

NPR Staff. 'More Fear of Human Intelligence than Artificial Intelligence in "Ex Machina".' *NPR*, 14 Apr. 2015. https://www.wnyc.org/story/more-fear-of-human-intelligence-than-artificial-intelligence-in-ex-machina/. Accessed 8 December 2018.

O'Hehir, Andrew. 'Dark Secrets of the Sex Robot: Alex Garland Talks A.I., Consciousness and Why "the Gender Stuff" of "Ex Machina" is Only One Part of the Movie's Big Idea.' *Salon*, 23 Apr. 2015, https://www.salon.com/2015/04/22/dark_secrets_of_the_sex_robot_alex_garland_talks_a_i_consciousness_and_why_the_gender_stuff_of_ex_machina_is_only_one_part_of_the_movies_big_idea/. Accessed 12 December 2018.

Onda, David. 'I Thought I Understood "Ex Machina" Until I Met Director Alex Garland.' *Xfinity*, 29 Apr. 2015. https://my.xfinity.com/blogs/movies/2015/04/29/i-thought-i-understood-'ex-machina'-until-i-met-director-alex-garland/. Accessed 8 Feb. 2019.

Ono, Kent A., and Vincent Pham. *Asian Americans and the Media*. Vol. 2. Polity, 2009.

Passary, Anu. 'Tinder Users at SXSW Fall for Ex Machina's Ava, But Here's What She Really Is'. *Tech Times*, 17 March 2015. https://www.techtimes.com/articles/40293/20150317/tinder-users-at-sxsw-fall-for-ex-machinas-ava-but-heres-what-she-really-is.htm. Accessed 12 Nov 2018.

Phillips, Ian. 'This Brilliant Sci-Fi Film is One of the Best Movies You'll See All Year.' *Business Insider*, 20 Apr. 2015. https://www.businessinsider.com/ex-machina-movie-review-2015-4. Accessed 27 September 2018.

Plaugic, Lizzie. 'Studio Promotes Ex Machina at SXSW with a Fake Tinder Account'. *The Verge*, 15 Mar. 2015. https://www.theverge.com/2015/3/15/8218927/tinder-robot-sxsw-ex-machina. Accessed 14 Oct. 2018.

Quirke, Antonia. 'Interview: Alex Garland on His New Venture "Ex Machina".' *Financial Times*, 16 Jan. 2015. https://www.ft.com/content/6955b908-9b35-11e4-b651-00144feabdc0. Accessed 2 February 2019.

Reyes, Mike. 'The Ex Machina Ending Debate: Is the Movie 3 Minutes Too Long?' *Cinema Blend*, 30 Apr. 2015, https://www.cinemablend.com/new/Ex-Machina-Ending-Debate-Movie-3-Minutes-Too-Long-71101.html. Accessed 4 October 2018.

Robbins, Martin. 'Artificial Intelligence: Gods, Egos, and Ex Machina.' *The Guardian*, 26, Jan. 2016, https://www.theguardian.com/science/the-lay-scientist/2016/jan/26/artificial-intelligence-gods-egos-and-ex-machina. Accessed 8 December 2018.

Robinson, Tasha. 'Alex Garland is Fine with Not Having Answers for Ex Machina's Questions.' *The Dissolve*, 8, Apr. 2015. https://thedissolve.com/features/interview/985-alex-garland-is-fine-with-not-having-answers-for-e/. Accessed 1 Jan. 2019.

Robinson, Tasha. 'Ex Machina.' *The Dissolve*, 9 Apr. 2015. https://thedissolve.com/reviews/1507-ex-machina/. Accessed 4 October 2018.

Russ, Joanna. 'The Image of Women in Science Fiction.' *Images of Women in Fiction: Feminist Perspectives*. Ed. Susan Cornillon. Bowling Green, OH: Bowling Green University Popular Press, 1972. 79-94.

Saito, Stephen. 'The Human Element: Oscar Isaac and Domhnall Gleeson Talk *Ex Machina*.' *Movie Maker*, 10 Apr. 2015. https://www.moviemaker.com/archives/interviews/the-human-element-oscar-isaac-and-domhnall-gleeson-talk-ex-machina/. Accessed 4 February 2019.

Saygin, Ayse Pinar, Ilyas Cicekli, and Varol Akman. 'Turing Test: 50 Years Later.' *Minds and Machines* 10, no. 4 (2000): 463-518.

Schwartz, Paula. 'Roundtable Interview: Alicia Vikander, Oscar Isaac Talk "Ex Machina" Robots.' *Reel Life with Jane*, 11 Apr. 2015. https://www.reellifewithjane.com/2015/04/roundtable-interview-alicia-vikander-oscar-isaac-talk-ex-machina-robots/. Accessed 22 January 2019.

Shanahan, Murray. 'What Do You Think About Machines That Think?' *Edge.org*, 21 Jan. 2015. https://www.edge.org/response-detail/26203. Accessed 1 November 2018.

Sikyta, Carsen. 'What's that Sound? Sound Design on Ex Machina.' *Vimeo*, 2 Feb. 2019, https://vimeo.com/165478693. Accessed 28 January 2019.

Sims, David. '*Ex Machina* Explores the Thrill (and Horror) of Romantic Uncertainty.' *The Atlantic*, 10 Apr. 2015. https://www.theatlantic.com/entertainment/archive/2015/04/ex-machina-review/390147/. Accessed 24 September 2018.

Smith, Nigel M. 'Alicia Vikander on Playing a Robot in "Ex Machina".' *IndieWire*, 10 Apr. 2015, https://www.indiewire.com/2015/04/alicia-vikander-on-playing-a-robot-in-ex-machina-63239/. Accessed 17 December 2018.

Snider, Eric. '12 Futuristic Facts about Metropolis.' *Mental Floss*, 25 Jul. 2016. http://mentalfloss.com/article/83617/12-futuristic-facts-about-metropolis. Accessed 12 January 2019.

Sofge, Erik. 'Lie Like a Lady: The Profoundly Weird, Gender-Specific Roots of the Turing Test.' *Popular Science*, 13 Jun. 2014. https://www.popsci.com/blog-network/zero-moment/lie-lady-profoundly-weird-gender-specific-roots-turing-test. Accessed 7 February 2019.

Thompson, A. '"Annihilation" Director Alex Garland Speaks Out on Screwing with Genre and Studio Panic Attacks.' *IndieWire*, 8 Apr. 2018, https://www.indiewire.com/2018/04/annihilation-director-alex-garland-devs-television-1201950154/. Accessed 6 September 2018.

Tellotte, Jay P. *Replications: A Robotic History of the Science Fiction Film*. University of Illinois Press, 1995.

Trendacosta, Katharine. 'The Easter Egg Hidden in *Ex Machina*'s Source Code. *i09*, 21 May 2015. https://io9.gizmodo.com/the-easter-egg-hidden-in-ex-machinas-source-code-1705972185. Accessed 7 November 2018.

Trikha, Ritika. 'The History of "Hello, World".' *HackerRank*, 21 Apr. 2015. https://blog.hackerrank.com/the-history-of-hello-world/. Accessed 20 February 2019.

Trunick, Austin. 'Domhnall Gleeson on "Ex Machina".' *Under the Radar*, 9 Apr. 2015. http://www.undertheradarmag.com/interviews/domhnall_gleeson_on_ex_machina/. Accessed 3 February 2019.

Vincent, James. 'Twitter Taught Microsoft's AI Chatbot to Be a Racist Asshole in Less Than a Day.' *The Verge*, 24 Mar. 2016, https://www.theverge.com/2016/3/24/11297050/tay-microsoft-chatbot-racist. Accessed 20 January 2019.

Wass, Janne. 'Captain Video and His Video Rangers.' *Scifist*, 11 Oct. 2015, https://scifist.wordpress.com/2015/10/11/captain-video-and-his-video-rangers/. Accessed 9 February 2018.

Watercutter, Angela. 'Ex Machina has a Serious Fembot Problem.' *Wired*, 9, April 2015. https://www.wired.com/2015/04/ex-machina-turing-bechdel-test/. Accessed 2 February 2019.

Williams, Casey. 'The Dark Meaning Behind the Word "Robot".' *Huffington Post*, 9 Apr. 2016. https://www.huffingtonpost.com/entry/meaning-word-robot_us_5706b66de4b0537661891e54. Accessed 10 October 2018.

Wilson, Natalie. 'How *Ex Machina* Fails to be Radical.' *Ms. Magazine*, 29 Apr. 2015. https://msmagazine.com/2015/04/29/how-ex-machina-fails-to-be-radical/. Accessed 14 Jan. 2019.

Y Combinator. 'Ex Machina's Scientific Advisor – Murray Shanahan.' *Y Combinator Blog*, 28 Jun. 2017, https://blog.ycombinator.com/ex-machinas-scientific-advisor-murray-shanahan/. Retrieved 17 September 2018.

Zhang, Baobao, and Allan Dafoe. 'Artificial Intelligence: American Attitudes and Trends.' *Available at SSRN 3312874*(2019).

www.ingramcontent.com/pod-product-compliance
Lightning Source LLC
Chambersburg PA
CBHW071414300426
44114CB00016B/2298